Block by Block

Piecing Together Central New Mexico's Past:

The Homesteaders

By Gail D'Arcy

Memoir
BOOKS
Chico, CA

Block by Block
Piecing Together Central New Mexico's Past:
The Homesteaders

First Edition

Cover photo of quilt by Laneé Lackey

ISBN 978-0-9793387-3-1
Library of Congress Control Number 2009932013

To contact the author or order copies of this book directly from her, phone Gail D'Arcy at (530) 532-1184, or e-mail gaildarcy@yahoo.com

Memoir Books
An Imprint of Heidelberg Graphics
2 Stansbury Court
Chico, California 95928

Contents

Remembering Cedarvale and Progresso in Central New Mexico 5

Before the Homesteaders 10

Introduction to Cedarvale 15

Histories of Residents in and around Cedarvale, New Mexico 23

Histories 36

The D. M. Allen Family 36
The Armon Austin Family 37
The Fred Belzer Family 40
Doyle Berryman 41
The David B. Campbell Family 42
The Candelaria Family 42
The Earl Chandler Family 43
The Asa Cathey Family 43
The Thomas Colbaugh Family 43
The Elcie Currents 44
The Elmer W. and Cecil B. (Pyburn) DeVaney Family 44
The Elmer DeVaney Family 45
Edna Dishman Tracey 45
The Foster Family 46
The Bennie Gallegos Family 47
Corine Lucero Gallegos 47
The William and Cora Gladwell Family and Uncle Wade Gladwell 48
The Charlie Gonce Family 49
The "Red" Goodwin Family 50
The Thomas A. Gregory Family 50
The Beryl Gustin Family 51
The Arthur R. Hamilton Family 52
The John Ellis Hamilton, Jr. Family 52
Judge Hamilton 54
W. T. Hesters 55
Daniel T. Hileman Family 55

Gladys Cawer Keelin 56
Paul Lackey Family 56
The W. D. Lackey Family 58
Cad C. Livingston Family 59
The Everett H. "Pete" McCloud Family 59
The Jack Mitchell Family 60
The Boyd Moseley Family 61
Maxine Pounds Brown 62
John W. Richardson and Family 62
- Background 62
- The Walton Family 63
- The Richardson Family 63

T. M. Richardson Family 65
Edna Robinson 65
Marie Zelpha Robinson 66
Oliver and Jettie Schneider 67
Clint Smith Family 68
The Harry Smith Family 69
Nora Smith 69
Tonkinson, M. P. Family 69
William C. Smith Family 70
Steiner, William Family 70
The Cad Stiggens Family 71
The Ramon Tenorio Family 71
Toombs, W. L. "Dub" 72
The Twyeffort Family 73
The Vickrey Family 77
- Nolan Vickrey 78

Clint Welch 78
Edna I. Wright 79
- Wright's Reunion 79

History of the Cedarvale Quilting Club 80
How To Make a Friendship Quilt 80

Progresso 87
B. E. Piggott Family 90
- About Mom (Della Piggott) 90
- Della's Wedding Dress 90
- Their Children: 94

Iva Humphries Hobbs 100
The Humphries 108
The Lackeys 117
- Lackeys and Owens 119

In Conclusion 120

Remembering Cedarvale and Progresso in Central New Mexico

By Gail D'Arcy

The stories of people who were early settlers to the New Mexico territory in the early 1900s weave together a fascinating saga of will and determination. This is a collection of histories written and told by the daughters, sons and grandchildren of those early settlers, most of whom were homesteaders. Homesteaders were pioneers who came by wagon and by railroad from nearby states, such as, Texas, Kansas, and Missouri, to claim sections (640 acres) and portions of sections made available by the federal government to those willing to live on and to improve the land (to "prove up" the claim, as they said). Many were lured to the land by railroad company promotions. Railroad companies, having laid miles of tracks to and around the New Mexico territory, needed customers/passengers to support these expenditures and so they advertised.

Many families, fathers and brothers and young sons, viewed this as a golden opportunity. This opportunity attracted proud, gentle, and hard working people who wanted to be independent and to provide for themselves and their children. By making a claim on soil that would "grow everything," men were willing to labor and endure hardships. These pioneers envisioned a land where they could work, worship, and establish their own communities and schools; where they could use their brains and their brawn to make life better and more wholesome for their families.

Another factor, which influenced many,

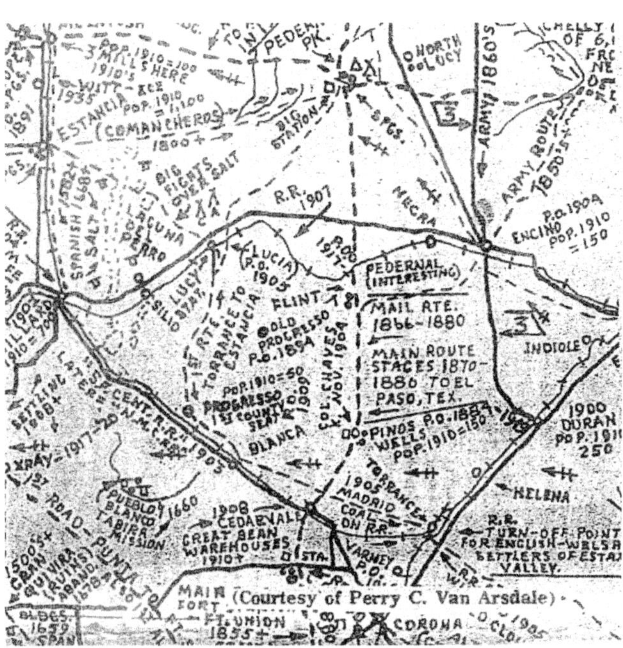

Map of Progresso/Cedarvale area. (Courtesy Perry C. Van Arsdale)

was the healthy climate. Because the New Mexico Territory was high and dry it was seen as a most very desirable location, especially for those suffering from respiratory ailments.

These industrious and adventurous individuals could not have known that to grow crops, graze livestock and sustain themselves, WATER was essential. Initially, it rained. Water was saved in cisterns. Some deep-water wells were dug with windmills delivering the water.

Barbed wire fences were strung. Plows pulled by horses or mules dug up the rich sandy soil.

The wind. The wind continued to blow. This may be the reason that the daughter of a homesteader once remarked, "a plow should never have been put to the soil."

The fine sandy loom "seemed to seep into and through everything." Of note are the stiff billed bonnets worn by the women and their daughters as they "hoed the beans"; an attempt to protect their faces from the constant blustery blasts of wind and the intense sunshine.

Life as a Homesteader

The people whose stories are being told here are those homesteaders who located in the central New Mexico areas from Estancia, through Willard and Progresso, to Cedarvale and Corona.

Personally, I am connected to these pioneers and to these stories because in 1913 my grandparents came from Kansas to homestead near Progresso. In about 1925, drought and lean times forced my grandparents, the Piggott's, to leave their homesteaded ranch and return to Kansas where Granddad worked for the railroad. In the 1950s after granddad retired, they returned to their New Mexico ranch. During this time, I spent my summers with them getting to be a part of the land and the people. I have learned much about the Cedarvale area from family connections, visiting with former residents, and because in 1985 I purchased the old Cedarvale Schoolhouse.

It is my intention that by piecing together the stories of those who lived in these areas of the New Mexico territory (New Mexico became a state in 1912) in the early 1900s, we can 'Block by Block'create a quilt-like pattern of friendship and cooperation.

Quilting. Quilting actually played a very big roll in bringing these early families together. Transportation was limited. Practicality was paramount. In 1916 a group of women began meeting in each other's homes every other Wednesday to piece together blocks of material scrapes to form quilts. Not only were these women able to make covers of warmth for their families, but also they were able to enjoy the company of others and to stay in touch. Often husbands provided transportation to these "quiltings" and participated in the noon potluck meals. In about 1953 when the Cedarvale School closed, the women continued their bimonthly Cedarvale Quilting Club (as the group had named themselves); meeting in the schoolhouse until, in the late 1970s, when "maintenance of the old building became too much for the husbands" and the Cedarvale Quilting Club moved to the Cedarvale Senior Center where they still meet. It is reported that the Cedarvale Quilting Club is the oldest continuously meeting quilting club in the United States.

In 1913, my grandfather, Bert Edgar Piggott, his wife Della and their two children, Verne who was two years old and my mother, Jeannette, who was three months old came by train to the little town of Progresso. In the beginning they leased land from others who had made claims on the land to be homesteaded. It appears that this was not unusual. Many people made claims and either were unable to improve the claims, as some had filed numerous claims in the names of their parents or other persons who never intended to live or work on the claims, or for one reason or another decided to lease their properties. My grandparents improved the land and eventually bought the land consisting of approximately two and one-fourth sections or 1,440 acres.

Their closest neighbors with adjoining property were the John Humphries. Their arrival is best described in the following quote of one of their daughters, Grace Humphries Lackey, who writes: "Papa came to New Mexico in 1909, it was a territory. He filed on a claim then went back to Kansas. In August 1910 he moved his family to New Mexico by train. The neighbors were at the depot in Progresso to meet them with wagons and moved them to the homestead, about two and a half miles south of Progresso. They put up a large tent and fixed a bed so my sick mother could rest. In the fresh air and sunshine, she soon recovered and lived seventeen years." The story has been told that Mrs. Humphries was carried there on a stretcher because her health was so poor.

These two families were very close. The children grew up together; worked and played and went to school. In about 1916, "a log schoolhouse was built in the center of the community." Probably the center of the community would have been at the corner of granddad's place, the Piggott Ranch.

This was life in Progresso. In a picture dated July 4th 1917, there is a rather large gathering of nicely dressed residents who had gathered for a holiday picnic. It has been told to me that frequently for special occasions, such as, Independence Day, relatives who had remained back home came by train to be part of the homesteaders gala events.

The closest large town (to Progresso) was Willard. Apparently, at one time, Willard was the county seat until "some fellows from nearby Estancia come and stole the railroad car that *was* the county office"; "they gave up without resistance since they were outnumbered." (Read more about Progresso people in a section to follow).

Separated by only about fifteen miles was another thriving independent community, that of Cedarvale. The story of Cedarvale is that it was founded in 1908 by homesteaders Ed Smith, William Taylor and Clinton P. DeWolfe. Cedarvale was comprised of forty acres and named after Cedarvale, Kansas. Soon there were three bean elevators, at least two grocery stores and other businesses with a population as high as three to five hundred people and a one-room schoolhouse. When Mr. DeWolfe donated twenty addition acres of his own land in 1917, Mr. L. O. Foster who was then the clerk of the local school board went before the Torrance County School Board to request a $5,000 bond be issued for the purpose of building a schoolhouse. Permission was granted and the schoolhouse consisting of four large classrooms was constructed between the years 1917–1921.

A lot happens in the '20s and '30s. Drought happened. Many farmers had to leave their farms to be maintained by their wives and children while they sought work elsewhere. Some went to work for the WPA. It was at this time around 1936, when the nation's economy was suffering as well as the farmers and ranchers of central New Mexico, that the WPA built onto the existing Cedarvale Schoolhouse two more classrooms and a large mini-pit gymnasium (reference: Ghost Town Basketball by Steve Flores, 2006).

The largest town close to Cedarvale was Corona. So while the residents of Progresso journeyed to Willard, Cedarvale residents went to Corona.

It should be noted that even before the homesteaders started settling some of this areas, there were Spanish families already established and grazing thousands of sheep or cattle. Some were on Old Spanish Land Grants.

The communities were close knit. My mother told me once that when the midwife came to deliver a younger sister or brother, "it was in the middle of the night and we were told to walk to the Beedle's place (approximately one and a half miles) where we spent the rest of the night and went from there to school the next day."

The schools were most often the center of social activities.

In the large Cedarvale Schoolhouse activities such as school programs, church functions, dances, and once even, according to Armon Austin, donkey basketball took place. Quilts were displayed; and potlucks held.

Another social activity, which would bring the communities of Progresso and Cedarvale together, was climbing the Gallinas Mt. In one picture, the families of the Piggott's and the Humphries' are loaded up on the horse drawn hay wagon headed for the Gallinas. On this particular outing, the oldest Humphries boy, Roy, rode ahead to set up camp. The trip took two days; they traveled over and camped out the first day. The next day, they climbed the mountain and returned home. Roy happened upon some boys who lived at the foot of the mountain, the Lackey boys, whom he invited to join their outing. Quoting Grace Humphries Lackey, "After the crops were clean and laid by for harvest time Papa took us for an outing. In those days Mountain Climbing was one of the main sports. And who should arrive on the scene but the Lackey brothers to climb the mountain with us ... that is when I met Paul, our friendship continued, grew into a courtship and after I graduated in May, from high School at Willard. We were married November 4, 1934." The story is oft told by other members of the climbing party that Paul assisted Grace by having her hold onto a stick; it was the"stick" that united the communities and the quilters.

Saga Continues

My grandparents had leased their ranch and returned to Kansas in about 1925 where granddad worked as a machinist for the railroad. However, grandmother and the children spent summers in New Mexico, often staying with their neighbors, the Humphries. When granddad retired around 1952, they returned to the Ranch to live.

My summers, during the 1950s, with the grandparents were busy and wonderful times; frequently other cousins joined us. We helped granddad clean up the old barn and tend the few animals they were raising. We helped the neighbors brand the cattle, played with other neighbor's kids while the older folks played pitch and "42," learned to drive the old Chevy pick-up, went to church, visited Indian Ruins, practiced shooting the .22 rifle, rode old "Smokey" and, of course, climbed the Gallinas. They were wonderful times for me and for my cousins. Modern conveniences were few; outdoor toilet (two-holer), water came from the hand pump outside, bathing was once a week (Saturday, of course) in a wash tub on the kitchen floor, telephone reached a handful of neighbors, only; heady stuff for us city dwellers.

I was very proud of my grandfather. His reputation for being an honest 'man of his word' was still intact. Granddad had a strong Christian belief and arranged to have Sunday preaching in the little old framed one-room schoolhouse/church on their property. We went with Grandmother to quilting on Wednesdays; she loved to sew and crochet and made beautiful things.

At some point in time, long ago, grandmother planted Lilac bushes at the entrance to their little homesteader's house, now ...

The trunks may be gnarled
The leaves a bit dry
But the lilacs
Grandmother planted
Still bloom.

And the wind blows and the air is still clear.
Where the sunrises and sets in the most
beauteous of ways,

This is our land, the Enchanted Land of Central
New Mexico.

Hope that you will enjoy reading about the lives and stories of persons who have been gracious enough to take the time and to remember just how it was when our land was being settled by a remarkable group of pioneers.

Lilac bushes in front of B.E. Piggott's Homesteaded Home (Photo taken by Gary D. Atkinson, 2006)

Before the Homesteaders

While I was learning about the history of the homesteaders in New Mexico, I realized that the "enchanted land" which I have come to love has a long list of inhabitants. It seems important to me to give the reader a little taste of the land and former inhabitants with the hope that appetites will be wetted to learn more about this amazing history. It was interesting to me that Water or the lack of water, has frequently been at the center of people having to change or abandon their ways of living.

NEW MEXICO:

Has 80 million acres; 121 square miles
It's the fifth largest state in the U.S.
It achieved statehood in 1912, second to last of the lower 48
It has more than 30,000 archeological sites including:
Pueblo Bonito at Chaco Canyon
Tyuonyi in Bandeleir
Quari and Gran Quivira
Manuelito Canyon
Galisteo Basin District,
Noted Pueblos: She' and Colorado

We are talking about cultures that existed long long ago. Pretty amazing stuff. It would seem appropriate to take a look at the New Mexico landscape and some of the cultures that have inhabited these lands.

"No one knows when the first nomadic families came because evidence of their passing is scant and difficult to date accurately (referring to the most recent and current Ice Age or glacial advance which ceased approximately 10,000 years ago and thus began the interglacial [glacial retreat] phase which we are now experiencing.) However, by:

• *10,000 BC "Clovis"*

Paleo-Indian people of the Clovis period inhabited the high mesas around Albuquerque, Clovis lived at the end of the Ice Age * coexisting with mammoths, saber-toothed tigers, and the formidable dire wolf; they traveled in small family bands, camping for days or weeks and, then, moving on to fresh hunting grounds.

• *9,000–8,000 BC "Folsom"*

Climate softened. Many animals became extinct and herds of giant bison roamed rich grasslands along the Rio Grande River. Along with the bison came hunters of the Folsom period. Folsom people camped along the high west mesa between Bernalillo and Los Lunas the Rio Rancho site, now an area of housing developments, is the only excavated Folsom period campsite in Northern America.

• *6,5000 BC "Cody"*

Giant bison vanished; climate became warmer and dryer, large herds of smaller bison filled eastern New Mexico grasslands. Buffalo hunters arrived; enter the Cody period.

"Eden" lance heads, dagger-like stone

blades, wicked stabbing tools, were introduced.

• *5,000 BC "Classic"*

Hunting society transformed into an "archaic" lifestyle New Mexico was hot; water was scarce.

Bison or buffalo herds retreated to the nation's northern plains and Classic hunting society became an Archaic lifestyle that foraged for small game and wild plant foods. Population increased, home territories decreased and family camps were inhabited for longer periods. Prior to the development of pottery, clay lined baskets were filled with water, then red hot cobbles were tossed in; food could be boiled.

• *1000 BC*

Villages of "pithouses" sprang up. Population continued to increase. Small cobbed corn was grown.

• *3000 BC–100 AD "Anasazi, Mogollon, Hokokam"*

Cultures settled in the Southwest and overlapping in the four corners with Utah and Colorado with the Fremont Indians.

All were similar but with their own distinct languages.

Agriculture increased with the growing of corn, beans, squash. Anasazi built massive stone structures in Chaco Cyn and Mesa Verde. Today's Southwest Pueblo Indians are direct descendents of the Anasazi. Around 100 AD, Anasazi, the Ancestral Puebloans, settled in the four corners area.

• *500 BC–500 AD*

Albuquerque's west mesa near Corrales was one of the more populated areas.

• *1–750 AD "Basketmaking Phase"*

Anasazi live in pithouses, started basket making. By 500 AD basketmakers lived in larger villages, built storage bins to hold corn. In addition to corn and beans, diet consisted of pinion nuts, yucca fruit, berries and wild game. Anasazi continued to hunt and gather to supplement the cultivated crops, maintained by dry farming and some flood irrigation. By 600 AD, farming was the mainstay. Pottery making began to be used to store excess crops and foods.

• *750–1300 AD "Pueblo Phase"*

Pueblo refers to an Indian culture not a particular tribe and is unique to the southwest. During this period cotton cloth, above ground housing and improved pottery came about. Around 750 AD Ancestral Puebloans started to build Chaco Canyon.

Trade was established with Mesoamerican Indian tribes of Mexico.

• *800–1000 AD*

Ancestral Puebloans spread over every arable acre of the San Juan Basin, more than 10,000 separate villages were established.

The "public architecture," as Chaco Canyon has been described, was built over decades.

• *1130 AD*

Chaco Canyon Society began to unravel. Began with a drought.

Around 1276, another drought caused the cliff dwellers of the four corners area to move; lack of water, famine, disease and raids by marauding nomads contributed to this disintegration.

• *1300 AD*

San Juan Basin completely abandoned

Moving rapidly along ...

• *1540*

Spanish Explorer, Francisco Vasquez de

Coronado explores New Mexico seeking the Seven Cities of Cibola (Gold). Fought with Zuni Indians.

- ***1598***

Juan de Onate' of Spain ordered by the king to New Mexico to spread Catholicism and build missions. More fighting.

The first Spanish speaking colony was established at San Juan.

- ***1610***

Governor Pedro de Peralta established Santa Fe.

- ***1680***

The Pueblo Riots. Taos Pueblo riots against the Spaniards, after years of religious persecution and drought.

Lead by a Puebloan named Pope, the Spanish flee to Santa Fe.

- ***1692***

Diego de Vargas reconquers New Mexico for Spain.

- ***1810***

Mexico's struggle for independence from Spain, begins.

- ***1821***

Mexico wins its independence from Spain; New Mexico becomes a province of Mexico; William Becknell opens the Santa Fe Trail, tying the southwest to the United States.

- ***1846***

American General Stephen W. Kearny took possession of New Mexico during the war with Mexico.

- ***1846–1848***

Mexican American War.

- ***1848***

New Mexico ceded to the United States in the Treaty of Guadalupe Hildalgalgo.

- ***1850***

Congress created the Territory of New Mexico.

- ***1851***

Bishop Jean Baptiste Lamy arrives in New Mexico; Catholic Priest who establishes the first English speaking school in Santa Fe.

- ***1853***

New Mexico acquired part of the Gila Valley through the Gadsden Purchase.

- ***1861–1865***

Civil War.

- ***1862***

Battle of Velarde, February 20–21, Confederate troops defeat Union troops; Battle of Glorieta Pass March 26–28 Union troops defeat Confederate troops.

- ***1862***

Homesteaders Act passed; encouraging "yeoman farmers" to develop and farm vast unclaimed lands.

- ***1863–1868***

Imprisonment of the Navajo and Mescalero Apaches at Bosque Redondo after "Long Walk"; many die.

- ***1863***

New Mexico Territory partitioned in half; Arizona created.

- ***1880***

The railroad arrives in New Mexico; opening up full-scale trade and migration from the East and Midwest.

• *1900*

With the arrival of the railroads, "the iron horse."

Homesteading begins in New Mexico ...

HOMESTEAD ACT

The Homestead Act was a United States federal law that gave one quarter of a section of a township (160 acres, or about 65 hectares) of undeveloped land in the American West to any family head or person who was at least twenty-one years of age, provided he lived on it for five years and built a house of a minimum of 12 by 14 feet (3.6 x 4.3 m), or allowed the family head to buy it for $1.25 per acre ($0.51/ha) after six months. To avoid penalizing men who were serving in the army, the length of military service was deducted from the required five-year residence period for veterans. [1] <http://skyways.lib.ks.us/towns/Hope/history.html> The act liberalized the homesteading requirements of the Preemption Act of 1841.

The act was signed into law by President Abraham Lincoln on May 20, 1862.

Background

The "yeoman farmer" ideal was a powerful ideal in American political history, and plans for expanding their numbers through a homestead law were agitated in the 1850s. The South resisted, fearing the increase in free farmers would threaten plantation slavery.[l] Two men stand out as greatly responsible for the passage of the Homestead Act: George Henry Evans and Horace Greeley. Agitation for free land started in 1844. Several bills were introduced unsuccessfully until 1862. After the South seceded and their delegations left Congress in 1861, the way was clear, and the act was passed.

By the end of the 19th century, over 570 million acres (2,300,000 km^2) remained open to settlement, but very little of this was usable for agriculture. As the frontier moved west onto the arid Great Plains, the amount of land a homesteader was allowed to claim was changed to 640 acres (2.6 km^2), a full section.

In Wyoming, Montana, and Colorado, homesteading cut into the access of the large ranches to water. In response, ranchers (themselves or their cowboys) homesteaded prime spots to reserve water access. At times, tensions escalated into violent conflicts called range wars, for example, the Johnson County War in Wyoming.

Results

The Homestead Act helped settlers create more than 372,000 farms. By 1900, the settlers had filed 600,000 claims for more than 80 million acres (320,000 km2) of land in the west under the Homestead Act. The leading historian Paul Gates has concluded, "their noble purpose and the great part they played in enabling nearly a million and half people to acquire farm land, much of which developed into farm homes, far outweigh the misuse to which they were put."

The first claim under the Homestead Act was made by Daniel Freeman for a farm near Beatrice, Nebraska on January 1, 1863; the site is preserved as the Homestead National Monument of America.

In 1871, 29,000 claims were made in Kansas under the Homestead Act. By 1886, this number had leaped to 43,000 claims.

The Federal Land Policy and Management Act of 1976 ended homesteading; the government believed that the best use of public lands was for them to remain in government control. The only exception to this new policy was in Alaska, for which the law allowed homesteading until 1986.

The last claim under the Homestead Act was made by Kenneth Deardorff for 80 acres (32 hectares) of land on the Stony River in southwestern Alaska. He fulfilled all requirements of the Homestead Act in 1979, but he did not actually receive his deed until May 1988. Therefore, he is the last person to receive the title to land claimed under the provisions of the Homestead Act.

Fraud and Corporate Use

The intent of the Homestead Act was to grant land for agriculture. However, in the arid areas west of the Rocky Mountains, 640 acres was generally too little land for a viable farm (at least prior to major public investments in irrigation projects). In these areas, homesteads were instead used to control resources, especially water. A common scheme was for an individual acting as a front for a large cattle operation to file for a homestead surrounding a water source under the pretense that the land was being used as a farm. Once granted, use of that water source would be denied to other cattle ranchers, effectively closing off the adjacent public land to competition. This method could also be used to gain ownership of timber and oil-producing land, as the federal government charged royalties for extraction of these resources from public lands. On the other hand, homesteading schemes were generally pointless for land containing "locatable minerals," such as gold and silver, which could be controlled through mining claims and for which the federal government did not charge royalties.

There was no systematic method used to evaluate claims under the Homestead Act. Land offices would rely on affidavits from witnesses that the claimant had lived on the land for the required period of time and made the required improvements. In practice, some of these witnesses were bribed or otherwise collaborated with the claimant. In any case the land was turned into farms.

Other acts

In 1906, the Forest Homestead Act was passed The Homestead Act of 1912 reduced the homestead requirement from five to three years.

Although a few isolated pockets remained into the 1950s, most of the desirable land in the lower 48 states had been taken up by 1910 or so. Homesteading continued on a small scale in Alaska until 1986.

International Derivations

The act was later copied with some modifications by Canada in the form of the Dominion Lands Act. Similar acts—usually termed the Selection Acts—were passed in the various Australian colonies beginning in New South Wales. [Source: *Wikipedia.*]

Introduction to Cedarvale

In my opinion, the residents of the areas around Progresso, Willard, Cedarvale and Corona, New Mexico, consisting mostly of homesteaders, were very intelligent individuals who believed in educating themselves and their children. They, also, expected their children to work hard and to adopt their philosophies, faiths, and endeavors. So, it is not surprising that over the years as drought occurred and it became necessary for families to move or to work out of the area, that the cohesive communities that were once necessary for survival became separated. As these children became adults, they realized just how valuable was their heritage.

So that when former Cedarvale residents got together every two years, they had the opportunity to reminisce. Usually someone at a reunion or at the Quilting Club would press individuals to record their family histories.

In addition to the personal histories, research at the Santa Fe museums and libraries have provided more information. People at the Senior Centers in Estancia and in Corona have provided additional "facts."

"Facts" are not always the same. It became clear that even interviewing the same person on different days, might yield different information; so some "facts" were not necessarily true. This was found to be so in the booklet entitled The History of Torrance Co. Some of the dates stated by older Cedarvale residents did not always agree with those found in the Archives. But, by and large, one can begin to imagine life as it was for the courageous people settling the New Mexico lands. From these stories of friendships and hardships, the reader can begin to piece together a lovely quilt of the homesteaders' lives block by block as they were in Central New Mexico 100 years ago.

Another source of information obtained from descendants of the Cedarvale area is a project with the New Mexico Farm and Ranch Heritage Museum of Las Cruces called the "Cedarvale Project." Several persons familiar with Cedarvale have been interviewed and their recollections recorded. Interspersed throughout the collection of Cedarvale histories are abstracts from these interviews. This organization's cooperation and contributions have been most valuable.

As much as has been possible, I have tried to copy the original manuscripts as they were written.

Beginning with the schoolhouse, the Cedarvale School, often the center of Cedarvale happenings.

Copies from the archives:

1) 1909, Cedarvale requests a new school district be created, see: School District No. 35, "Cedarvale"
2) 1910 Schoolteachers; one-room schoolhouse
3) Mountainaire, New Mexico, August 25, 1917, The County Board of Education, Torrance County.

L.O. Foster clerk of School Board of District #35 requests permission to issue $5,000 bond, monies to build school; approved. Original four large classrooms built.

4) July 22, 1918, county board delegates

local school board #35 to "look after" schoolhouse construction.

5) Torrance County School Board Minutes (typed) June 30, 1921, "ordered advertisement be made for completion of #35 school building."

School District No. 35.
"Cedarvale."

A petition for a new school district having been received and filed in this office, same signed by requisite number of petitioners, and bearing requisite number of names of children of scholastic age residing there: therefore I create Cedarvale District No. 35 with boundaries as follows:

Beginning at the government corner stone on the base line, between townships Nos. 1N, 10E and 1N, 11E, N.M.P.M., thence north eighteen (18) miles, thence east six (6) miles, thence south six (6) miles thence east six (6) miles, thence south twelve (12) miles thence west twelve (12) miles, to point of beginning.

The following directors are appointed for said district:

John M. Dunn.
Benj. L. Howell
Albert Hall.

Mountainair, N.M.
April 10, 1909.

Chas. L. Burt.
Supt. of Schools

Document copies courtesy of Fray Angelico Chavez History Library and Photo Archives, Santa Fe, N.M.

Dist No	Name		Post Office	Elected	Appt'd
33	J. R. Williams.		Mountainair		5-2-10
	Peter Smith		"		5-2-10
	Robert Henley		"		5-2-10
34.	R. W. McCoombs	P	Mountainair	4-4-10	
	J. B. Hall	C		4-4-10	
	R. Sellers			4-4-10	
35.	C B Smith	Pres	Cedarvale	4-4-10	
	J H Padgett	C		4-4-10	
	[illegible]			4-4-10	
36.	J. H. Flowers	P	McIntosh	4-4-10	
	J. H. Lynch	C	"	4-4-10	
	John Gloss			4-4-10	
37.	M. Jenkins	C	Mountainair		5-2-10
	J. A. Cooper				5-2-10
	A M Tate				5-2-10
38.	J. R. Rhoades	P	Mountainair		5-24-10
	D. H. Thomas	C			5-24-10
	J. H. Irwin	D.			5-24-10
39.	J. F. Snow	P	Estancia		6-10-10
	W. M. Brooks	C	Willard		6-10-10
	G. C. Powell				6-10-10
40	W. L. Clifton	P.	McIntosh		9-3-10
	A. Eblen	C			9-3-10
	Mrs C. D. Kellog				9-3-10
41	Loyd Blevins	P	Progreso		[illegible]
	D. Delaney	C			
	W J Hurst	D			

Mountainair N.M. 8/25-17

The County Board of Education met at call of President. Members present Julius Meyers Alejandro Baca and W R Orme. Chas L Burt presiding.

J. C. Webb appeared in behalf of Dist # 30 asking for improvements in heating system and completion of ceiling in School building in that district. Directors of that district were authorized to put in one stove to be used for this session of school. They were also authorized to put ceiling on the rooms and purchase one Chair for use of the teacher at a cost of 3.85 plus freight from Topeka Kansas.

L. O. Foster Clerk of Board of Dist # 35 appeared asking for the approval of this Board of their action in issuing Bonds in the sum of $5000.00 for the purpose of raising money to erect a School building in that district. In this Connection the following resolution was adopted –

"In the matter of the Bond issue of school Dist #35 Torrance County, New Mexico, It appearing that a question having arisen as to the authority of the Dist Board in reference to the issuance of bonds, the following resolution is hereby passed by the County Board of Education in session at the office of the County Superintendant of Schools this 25th Day of August, 1917."

Be it Resolved:– That the action of the school Board of School District No 35, Torrance County, New Mexico, in calling in Calling an election for the purpose of voting on the question of bonding the district in the sum of five thousand Dollars for the purpose of erecting and furnishing a School house in said District is hereby approved, and any all actions taken by said board of directors is also hereby approved"

Signed: Chas. L. Burt. Pres. C.B. of E.
W. R. Orme Sec C.B. of E.

Owing to representations of directors of school Districts Nos 26 + 35 their districts were granted permission to begin their schools on the 3rd Monday in October instead of the First Monday, as School Buildings were not ready.

District No. 16 was allowed all small items needed in getting ready for school, but Piano was disallowed.

District No 4 was allowed 20 seats of Medium size.

The Contest in Dist No 44 as to legality of directors, being brought before this Board, the directors appointed by the superintendant was recognized as the legal board of directors of said district.

Mountainair N.M. 7/22-18

The County Board of Education met at office of County School Superintendant of Education. Chas. L. Burt presiding. Members present C.M. Milburn and W R Orme.

Resolution passed delegating to local boards to look after the construction of school buildings in Districts 8, 28 + 35 and County Superintendant was instructed to write letters of authority to these boards.

County superintendant was authorized to check the account of Nellie Bigbee and issue a duplicate warrant in case the original has been lost.

Report of Superintendant Burt on purchase of an adding Machine at a cost of 131.50 was approved and he was instructed to issue warrant in payment for same.

It was ordered that if District #30 shows enumeration of 51 that the County Superintendant be authorized to provide another teacher.

Two Members of local board of ~~District No 12~~ ~~were~~ present asking permission to put ~~on~~ a teacher in that part of district known as "Frontier". It was left to the local bard to work out the question.

District #44 were again represented before the Board, and the County superintendant was instructed to write to District Attorney to get an order from the Court instructing the local board of that district to rebuild the school house at the site first selected, and have it ready for the coming term term in 1918.

The Bills as follows were allowed:

O A Matson & Co $10.90. Ramundo Romero 25.65 - latter to be paid when oKd by local board who created the indebtedness. Great American Insurance Company 154.00. C M Milburn 4.80 W R Orme 2.50

County School Superintendant was authorized to order flags of the U.S. and necessary seats for the schools of the County not to exceed one car load.

Adjourned to meet August 26th 1918.

W. R. Orme
Secretary

Chas L Burt
President

Minutes of Meeting of June 30th, 1921.

At a regular meeting of the Board of Education of Torrance County, New Mexico, duly held at the office of the Co. Supt. of Schools of said County at the Court House, pursuant to call and notice by Supt., present the President of said Board, Mrs. Blanche Parrett, Ralph G. Roberson, Secretary, and Roy Brown and T. V. Ludlow, members, constituting the whole board, the following proceedings were had, to-wit:

Ralph G. Roberson elected Secretary and Manuel d' A. Otero, elected Vice President.
Minutes of May 20, 1921, read and approved.
Sch. Dist. #1. allowed $200.00 out of 1920 budget to repair and change building under supervision of this Board and be allowed a 2nd teacher for coming school year.
Motion carried that Superintendent advertise for bids for 4-room school house in Sch. Dist. 2 the balance of the cost over amount now available to be raised by special levy on property in said District.(Examination of premises on the 1st of July by the Board fixed site for same).
Sch. Dist 44 asked to present a petition of the citizens thereof as to where their School Bldg. should be located.
Motion carried that County Board will maintain an additional School in Scholl District No. 30, if said District will furnish the building.
Motion carried that available funds of Sch. Di t.16 be used under the supervision of the Supt. for the purchase of equipment for said district.
Ordered that advertisement be made for completion of School Bldg. in School District No. 35.
Superintendent asked to write Sch. Board of Sch. Dist. #13 asking what provision has been or will be made to take care of children of school age in said district near the line of Sch. Di st #4.
Motion carried that Sch. Dist. #5 be allowed two teachers.
Superitendent ordered to advertise for bids for repairing Sch. Bldg. in #10.
Suberitendent instructed to ntofy #12 to repair building and that expense therefor be paid out of the funds now on hand of said district.
Resolution adopted calling election to vote bonds in Sch. Dist. 15 for Aug. 15, 1921, on motion of Roy Brown and second by T. V. Ludlow, all voting in favor. (See resolution).
Mtion carried that the School house in SD 17 be moved to present building site of proposed new School house and, under supervision of the Superintend of this Board repairs be made to suit present necessities for coming term.
Motion carried that Lucy truck line be extended to take on 9 children from Sch. Dist. 43, said children from #43 being hereby ordered to Lucy.
Ordered that Superintendent ask Sch. Dist. 28 for estimate and specifications repairs Old Bldg. and making proposed cistern.
Superintendent asked to again take up the matter of consolidation of Sch. Dist #40 Torrance County with Chilili Distrtict Bernalillo County with the school authorities at Albuquerque.
Motion carried that provision be made for transporting 9 children from out of NW Cor. Sch. Dist. 35 to School in District 45.
Motion carried that truck Supt. purchase necessary repairs for Ford trucks and fix them up.
Motion carried that Sch. Dist. #46 use of funds now on hand sufficient to equip Sch. building and a levy is ordered 5 mills for building a school house, to be expended under supervision of the Superintendent of Schools.
Motion carried that Fed. Chavez be paid $120.00 for year's rental next term of his building in Sch. Dist. 48 provided he, before commencement of school, repair said building to satisfaction of County Supte of Schools.
School building for Dist. 51 denied.
Bills approved and paid as follows:

Estancia Auto Co. $	$4.20
do	14.20
Estancia Valley Sup. Co.	5.31
Estancia Auto Co.	11.09

Bill from #43 passed for investigation. This bill $63.00-
Motion carried that Supt. transfer from Rural Sch. Fund sufficient to balance institute fund.

The old Cedarvale schoolhouse, Cedarvale, N.M., 2006. (courtesy G. D. Atkinson)

SCHOOL

The country school
The golden rule
The thing that I recall
T'was the big round clock ... upon the wall
Dust mop odor on hardwood floors
First time I recall seein'
Long skinny corridors
As well as double open doors
If I could be the one, Oh the chosen one
My heart would fill with pride
To dust those chalk erasers ... outside
Those days seem so long ago

excerpts from the poem "School" by Bobby Neeley, June '07

2007 schoolhouse in front and out back

Histories of Residents in and around Cedarvale, New Mexico

Helen Foster Toland, daughter of F. O. Foster and a retired schoolteacher, collected these histories in 1982; she wrote the following.

Cedarvale, New Mexico was founded in 1908 before New Mexico was a state. It consisted of a plot of ground of forty acres.

It had names of streets designated but few people know what they are. Streets running north and south are Cedar Avenue, Main Street, Popular Avenue, and Walnut Avenue. Those running east and west are First Street, Second Street, Third. Street, and Fourth Street.

Edward L.Smith, L. W. DeWolf and Mr. Taylor were those who laid out the town site. The area the school is in was donated by L. W. DeWolf and is not in the forty acres.

Mrs. L. W. DeWolf was the first postmistress with the first post office being established in 1909.

This group of family histories was put together by Helen Foster Toland. It is not typed in the very best way as I am no accomplished typist. If there are errors I apologize. I am sure there are quite a few histories omitted which should have been included but these are all I have been able to obtain.

As you will see, these were hardy people who settled this area. Had this not been such a dry region, it would have been a far different story today.

The following people now reside in Cedarvale. They are Ramon Tenorio and his wife, Mary Ann, Loy Robinson and his wife, Marie, Hazel Bickford, Edward Lopez and family, and Pauline McCloud.

There is no longer a post office or store or business of any kind. There is a senior center which is very active and as a part of it, the Quilting Club which had its early beginnings in 1916 when the members met in homes. Today, Cedarvale is getting quite a name for itself because of the beautiful quilts that are still made by its members.

After almost completing this work, a copy of life in this area as recorded by Mrs. Lula F. Kendall came into my possession. It is so outstanding describing pioneer life that I felt that it should be included here. Allison Kendall Cummins gave permission to use it.

Helen Toland at home in Roswell, 2008. (courtesy Brandon Blankenship)

One of several Cedarvale School drawings by Tonya and Kay Laubach

Some of the people who taught at Cedarvale School

Annamell Austin
Boucher, Archie and Inez
Boucher, Henry and Madeline
Belzer, Buelah
Caster Emmett
Mrs. Cravens
Mr. Blakely
Bernice Donaldson
Blanch Davis
Addie Dennis
Davis, Mable
Elbert Ernest
Foster, Vera
Mrs. L.G. Foster (the first teacher)
Viva Goodner
Effie Harris
Vires Holman
Gertrude Hughes
Mr. Ham
Mrs. Jensen
Clara Meyers
P .L. Mitchel
Hazel Moore
Miss Nelligan
Lois Newberry
Annie Ramsey
Lena Sanders
Fern Shaw
J.C. Shaw
W.K. Twyeffort
Mrs. Torrance
Grace Taylor
Faye Terry
Mary Ann Tenorio
Mrs. Ward
Mr. and Mrs. Bob Weeks
Ida Mae Welch
Noel Wallace
Mrs. Vonde
Mrs. Vigil

Six Years on a Claim in New Mexico

By Lula F. Kendall

Cedarvale, New Mexico

In presenting this, a true story of my life for the past six years, to the public, I do so at the request of a dear friend and relative who, on November 13, 1920, "crossed over the border." This lady, Mrs. Adona H. Galbraith of Elvaston, Illinois, was a cousin of my mother. She has been a great comfort and assistance to me, both mentally and financially, and to her memory, I dedicate this, my effort to fulfill her request.

Thirteen years after our marriage, my husband concluded, with our growing family, there was no chance to achieve anything outside a living as a wage earner. Our little home in north central Texas was sold, and he boarded the train for the West. March 16, 1917, he filed on three hundred twenty acres homestead and three hundred twenty additional in the Estancia Valley at the foot of the Pinos Mountains, seven and one-half miles north of Cedarvale, New Mexico, a small town on the New Mexico Central Railroad.

April 3rd, we left with our family—three boys, ten, eight, and six years of age, one little three-year-old daughter and a baby girl of two months. We took household goods and enough clothing, we thought, to last the three years we would have to spend on our claim before getting our deed. Alas! Seventeen cars of the freight train on which our goods were shipped were completely demolished, and our possessions destroyed. In the meantime, our brother, A.T. Flowers, and two brothers-in-law, M.G. Koen and G.C.Worley, had come on ahead. Two of them had their houses built when we arrived, so we found a landing place while waiting for our household goods. My husband filed on a relinquishment, paying $400.00 for the improvements. Consisting of a heavy hewn log cabin, sixteen by sixteen, with side room, a dugout; lots and sheds built of logs and cedar posts set up, picket fashion, on the east side of the homestead. A half-dugout, sixteen by twenty, was on the west. One hundred sixty acres were fenced with two wires, and about forty acres were sod broken.

For nearly a month after we came, we waited for our household goods, before moving on to our claim, only to learn they were destroyed—furniture, dishes, cooking utensils, in fact, everything that could be mashed or smashed. Here we were, strangers in a strange country no teams, no farming implements, no wagons, nothing much even to "housekeep" and nowhere in reach to buy them. Seed to buy, feed to buy and a thousand other things. I had not wanted to come, but now that we were here, I decided to make the best of things. We scraped together every available thing, here and yonder, and moved on our claim the eighth of May.

Then began our hunt for teams. My husband and younger brother, (Manford D. Flowers, who with his young bride, moved here a few weeks after we came) rode for three weeks or more trying to find horses for sale. In the meantime, I was trying to clean and repair our house, and it was so dusty. I beat and broke out the sod and redobbed it with doby (adobe), which is white and clean looking. I painted the whole inside white with cold-water paint. With goods boxes of all sizes and cretonne, I manufactured dresser, washstands, closets, cupboards, medicine case and china closet. The old iron bedsteads we managed to secure were given two coats of white enamel. Chairs of different sizes were given a coat of light oak paint, then varnished, as were our dining table and small bookcase. With carpets, rugs and curtains saved from the wreck, our "shack on the claim" began to take on a cozy appearance.

The view of the Pinos Mountains from our front door is a lovely sight. Great towering pines and pinon cover. Rocks of all colors, shapes and sizes are there. The remains of an old silver mine can be seen. Large pieces of slate-colored rocks, studded with the shining ore, can be found scattered about the mine site. At the vase of the mountains and quite a distance around them cedars grow thickly.

Fifteen miles south are the Gallinas Mountains where the "homesteaders" go each season to hunt deer. I have been there only once, but I wish I could go often. Forty-five miles west are the Manzana Mountains. I have never been there, but can see them plainly from our home. (One hundred miles north can be seen the snow-caps of Colorado.) Our altitude is 6,400 feet. Corn, cane and pinto beans are common main crops at present. Some day this will be a fine grain country. There is no machinery to handle the grain now. We are within a day's drive by wagon to eleven different railroad towns, all small. Estancia, the county seat, is the largest.

In May, our father and stepmother, Mr. and Mrs. W. T. Flowers of Denton, Texas, came out to view the country. Another brother, Eldridge P. Flowers, the "old batch" of our family, filed here, so there are three families of us on the north of the mountains and three on the south. How fortunate for all we decided to alight close together. While our parents were here, we climbed mountains, sometimes taking lunches and making a day of it. We took all kinds of Kodak pictures.

Everything was new and strange. I felt as if I were a thousand miles from everywhere and would often slip out at night and gaze at the moon and stars, for they were all that seemed natural. Father was carried away with the country. So much so they came again in August.

The first year we did not get teams and tools in time to do our own planting but hired the work done. We made a short crop but got a good price for our beans, $8.50 and $9.00 per hundred. There was little fieldwork to do that year, so my husband dug a cistern, broke more sod, did more fencing and cut cedar post when not otherwise employed. That winter he hauled posts to Lucy, eighteen miles away, and traded them for groceries or such things as we needed which were available there.

I always dreaded to see him start. Our snowstorms came so quickly, and, oh, it can be so cold! I would begin looking for him late in the afternoon. Could see him after he had passed the Rattlesnake Knobs, eight miles northwest of us, if it wasn't too dark. I would look as long as daylight lasted then sit up to keep our fire going until he came in. Many nights I've waited until ten, eleven or twelve o'clock before he came in. And once it was two o'clock in the morning, but a hot fire was awaiting him when he came, almost frozen. No one but those who have gone through the same thing knows the mental suffering I endured. Once after that he was caught in a blizzard coming from Pedernal, ten miles north of us, with a load of feed and groceries. One of the horses had taken the colic. He was coming through the McDonald ranch where hundreds of cattle grazed and could not leave the wagon for the cattle would have destroyed everything. He stayed with his load until morning, with only one heavy quilt to wrap himself in. Early next day he rode in for another horse, leaving the wagon in the care of a ranch hand.

The second year we made only fair crops. Corn and cane did not mature well because of an early frost, and beans brought only six dollars per hundred.

All this time we had no school. I believe this worried me more than anything else. I had taken my children from a fine school and brought them to run wild. You never saw a happier set of boys. Mexican burros grazed the prairies in droves. My boys had never owned horses since they had always lived in town. Now they made good use of those burros. Many a time I've cringed and shut my eyes to keep from seeing them get their necks broken. But it was a joy for them, and the overalls I had brought to last for three years gave out in six months. They seldom put on a new pair that a burro didn't run or throw them into a wire fence. Oh, the uneasiness a mother of boys endures, especially a timid mother like myself! Today I am still as nervous about them, but breaking broncs is THE LIFE! Today I can't or won't watch them ride anything but their regular saddle horses.

But to get back to my subject. The second year we all felt we must have a school. Mrs. R. V. King, whose husband had bought the relinquished claim joining us on the south, agreed to teach in our half dugout for two dollars per scholar per month. We gave her the school. Our county superintendent, hearing of our efforts for a school, came down later and employed her for the rest of the school term.

On December 13, 1918, my husband loaded his wagon with one hundred pound sacks of beans and left for Corona, a town twenty-two and a half miles away. Returning with a load of groceries, he said, "Our blizzards will soon be coming, and I'm not going to take any chances of getting caught in them. We'll try to keep supplies ahead."

December 16th our first real snowstorm of the season came. The snow lay on the ground for fifty-six days. Our load of groceries was all that kept ourselves and our near neighbors from going hungry. Any other supplies my husband walked and carried in a towsack from Cedarvale, seven and a half miles away. The snow was so deep there was no going anywhere except on foot. It took him all day and until eight or nine o'clock sometimes to make the trip.

The snow was on a five foot level all over our yard except in a five or six foot space around our cabin where it had blown out. We melted snow each day to get water for ourselves and stock. The children and I filled our cistern with snow and had ice water until the latter part of June. The cold cracked the cement of the cistern so badly I've never tried it any more. Lots of cattle starved and froze to death that winter. And for the first and last time since coming here, we had no Christmas tree for the children of the neighborhood. For twenty-one days we had no mail because the trains could not reach Cedarvale for the snow drifts. When we did get it, a dozen men on foot met the train a mile and a half from town and carried in twenty-three mailbags. That night Mr. Kendall came in at nine o'clock with two towsacks filled with mail for us and neighbors.

During this snow, our relatives and neighbors on the other side of the mountains ran out of provisions. They were three and a half miles closer to Cedarvale then we were, but there was only a small store or two there at the time. We could get scarcely anything, a few canned goods, matches, coal oil and the like. Two of my brothers, Adron and Eldridge, and my brother-in-law, George Worley, walked to Cedarvale and in company with three or four neighbors boarded a railroad hand car and began their trip to Progresso to get groceries. It was about ten miles, but it took them all day and far into the night to make the trip. They brought back all they could load on the car. Such times I never saw before or since, yet in a way we all enjoyed it. Not one of us had even a bad cold.

During the first days of the snow, Mr. J. L. Draper, who then lived a mile north of us, came to borrow some flour. I told him I could let him have a fifty-pound sack if he wanted it. He replied, "Oh, no. Just give me a few pounds. I think we can get to town this week." But every few days he came trudging through the snow for more until, when he paid it back, he brought a fifty-pound sack. One sack I loaned three different times before it came home to stay. After the snow froze over, some of the men would lead a horse and walk to Cedarvale. They loaded a sack of flour (before the flour gave out there) or other groceries on the horse, walk and lead him back as it was too dangerous to ride. Some of the families did without a light for two or three weeks, but we did not. We use Aladdin lamps, and, when the oil began to get low, Mr. Kendall would put a quart bottle in each overcoat pocket and make another trip to Cedarvale.

In my family each holiday or birthday is usually celebrated differently from other days. But during that winter I would almost freeze when I went to the kitchen. So Christmas we had our usual late breakfast, and about four o'clock in the after noon I gave everybody cake and hot chocolate. The children seemed a bit disappointed, but I told them we would have a nice dinner on New Year's, even if we did have to eat it alone. Each day during the week I did some extra baking. New Year's arrived clear and cold with snow, snow everywhere. We slept late that morning as usual, and as I was sweeping the front room, I heard a great commotion. Glancing out, I saw my brother, sister and their families coming and shouting. Their children were all so pleased to get away from home and mine to have company. We did not have to eat our dinner alone. The severe cold lasted until the coming March.

The third year we made good crops, getting a little less for our beans but selling quite a bit of corn and cane to newcomers. We did more improving, got a school started right here in our midst, organized a literary society. We had spelling matches every Saturday night at the schoolhouse. Often we served fruit, chocolate and cake, or we would have a box supper after the spelling. Such fun as we had! Little, big, old and young were always there.

At Christmas we would have a program then the tree. On Mother's and Father's Day there would be another program, given out in the open under a brush arbor. People came from miles around, in cars, wagons, buggies, on horseback and on foot. At Easter there was an Easter egg hunt at the mountains and dinner on the ground.

A.J. Kirkpatrick, formerly of Olney, Texas, filed a claim three and one-half miles northwest of us. His wife was an accomplished pianist and sweet singer. Two of my brothers here are musicians. They play violin, banjo, guitar and mandolin, also trombone and cornet. Mrs. Kirkpatrick and my eldest sister, Mrs. Koen, were the only ones in our community who owned pianos. So our singing and fruit suppers we usually held at one place or the other. We had fruit suppers often that summer, each family taking along a cake and a can of fruit. There were also dances and ice cream suppers, everybody attending whether they danced or not.

Each summer there were visitors here, mostly from Texas, relatives and friends of the homesteaders. They often remarked, "You people have jolly times and get more fun out of life than anyone back home." But they were here only a few weeks out of each year. Our climate is really delightful through July and August when everything is burning up other places.

One summer D. B. Koen, a Primative Baptist minister from Wellington, Texas, visited his son here. He remarked one day he would like to preach to the people before he left. A night or two later there was a dance and ice cream supper at Adron's. People came from miles around. After it was over, Adron stepped outside and shouted, "Listen, everybody! Brother D. B. Koen will preach at the schoolhouse Saturday night, Sunday and Sunday night. Everybody come."

After the services, it was told as a joke, the minister at the close of the sermon said, "I may never meet with you people again. So, before I close these remarks, I wish to announce there will be a dance at G. C. Worley' next Thursday night. Everybody attend." Such is the spirit of the west. The people, as a rule, are frank, open and free-hearted; very little selfishness is known here. Someone is always willing and ready to help carry another's burden, when it grows too heavy to be carried alone.

Our third year, Professor W. St. Clair of Moriarty, New Mexico, taught our school. That winter was the mildest since our coming. Cold? Yes, but not continually away below zero. Then - - Sickness for the first time seized our neighborhood. I had studied Pharmacy myself. Before moving here I ordered a supply of medicine and sent it on in my sister's care. I, also, purchased quite a few remedies from our home drug store which can't be bought everywhere, so I was not caught napping when sickness came. But what a time I had, and so did others. The Flu, I suppose it was – anyway that's what we called it- first broke out. Everybody in the country had it. I could not depend on my relatives as they had all they could attend to at home. So I cared for my own family and my neighbors' families, too.

My sister, Mrs. Koen, had her family and Professor St. Clair, who boarded there, to care for. Yes, I had it myself, but I never gave up. Just had to keep going to care for my children. For three weeks I never slept a whole night's sleep. Shelton, my third boy, was first to fall ill. He was weakly anyway, and it came near running into Pneumonia. One by one, the children kept dropping out of school. Elton, my second boy, was last. He came in one evening. "Mamma," he said, " I'm sick, and Garvin (a neighbor boy) is sick, too, and had to leave school when I did." I put him to bed at once and began my treatment. In two days he was wanting to get up. Mr. Kendall was going to the McDonald ranch that morning and had to pass by Mr. Campbell's place. "Stop and see how Garvin is," I called. I hadn't heard from him since he left school.

He came back just as I was putting dinner on the table. Said he didn't go in, but Mrs. Campbell told him Garvin was getting worse and worse all the time. I know where my boy, who was begging to get up, would have been if I had not known how to care for him. "Here," I cried to by husband, "you finish getting dinner on the table and look after the children. I'm going to see Garvin."

He replied, "No. Just fix the medicine, and I will take it down there. You are worn out and sick yourself."

While he objected I was cramming medicine in my apron pockets and answered only as I went out the door. "Can't do it till I see what condition he is in."

Our homes are three quarters of a mile apart, but I was soon there, and what a condition I found the child in. As I stepped in the door, I asked, "How are you, Garvin?" (though well I knew). His mother replied, "He would answer you if he could, but he hasn't spoken a word for two days."

He was propped up on pillows to a sitting position, great drops of perspiration on face and brow, shoulders heaving, as he fought for breath. All over the place you could hear him trying to breathe. I gave him a dose of medicine (will not name it here as it is dangerous). Cut the end off a lemon and gave it to him to take his mind off his suffering as much as possible. Turning to his mother, I told her, "Give him another dose in thirty minutes if Dave (Mr. Kendall) or I is not back here, but keep it away from the children as it's a deadly poison."

Then I ran home as fast as my feet would take me. My husband had his team hitched to the wagon to go for a load of wood when I came in. I told him one of us had to go and stay with that boy or he would be dead before a doctor could reach him, and for him to go. I told him to give the medicine every fifteen minutes and stay right with him as I was afraid that when that membranous condition began breaking loose, he would choke to death, and I could not stand that. We lost our eldest child with diphtheria, and its agony to me to see any child choking. He went. Kenneth, my eldest living son, saddled his pony and left in a dead run for Cedarvale to phone for a doctor. He got Dr. Stone from Corona, then waited at Cedarvale for him to get there. Kenneth left his pony in Cedarvale and came on in the car with the doctor to show him the way. As I had expected, the membranous condition began giving away long before the doctor arrived, and the boy had to fight for his life. But, when Dr. Stone finally came, Garvin was talking. Dr. Stone told the Campbells their boy was now out of danger. All he needed was careful nursing.

A few days later, the whole family was sick with colds, sore throats, high temperatures, pains in the chest. Three of my family were ill, but I managed to partly care for them all. At night I would get my ill ones settled for the night, then fill my apron pockets with medicine and fever thermometer, carry a sack of cookies in my hand for the children who were better and go alone, on foot, to see how they were faring. Have found the mother when she couldn't speak above a whisper, her temperature above 104, and the father propped up in a rocker, struggling to breath. I would stay until their temperatures were on the downward march and make them as comfortable as possible for the night.

I have gone, sat up and doctored the sick until two or three o'clock in the morning, then come home alone, part of the way through timber, when I could hear the howl of the coyotes in the distance.

Afraid? No, but before coming here I couldn't have been hired to do such things. That winter I made quite a reputation as a doctor, and today those within two or three miles of us will send for me before sending for a physician, and often he is never called. Those who have cars come for me and bring me home. If close by, I usually walk.

Last summer, as I was cooking dinner, a car stopped at our gate, and a young man came to the kitchen door saying, "I have a prescription here I want to get you to fill."

Wondering who? Where? I opened the note, finding it was from my father, who that morning had gone to Cedarvale to catch the train to Santa Fe. Hearing one of the merchants (who had gone in business there long after we came) telling about his wife's being so sick, he told him to send to me for medicine that would relieve her. Well, the longest road always has a turning point, and that summer was, I believe, the jolliest time we have spent here.

Many were getting their deeds, and some were planning to leave. Quite a few visitors came for several weeks. W. H. Keen, who owns a farm and lovely home at Olney, Texas, having lost his wife a few months before, came out and filed on three hundred and twenty acres relinquishment so he could be near his daughter, Mrs. A. J. Kirkpatrick. He brought with him his two unmarried children, Miss Fay, a young lady of seventeen, like her sister an accomplished pianist, and Billie, as we all familiarly called him, a big over-grown lad of nineteen.

Such times as we had that summer! Plays, singings, dances, fruit and ice cream suppers and picnics. We had one picnic and chicken fry at the mountains that summer, R. V. King frying the chickens, a dozen or more, on a camp fire. They were simply fine. People came from thirty-five miles away, most all bringing well filled lunch boxes. C. E. Biglow, then cashier of the Estancia Saving Bank, came with his family and distributed freely pencils, candy and cigars. Mrs. Koen's piano was loaded on a wagon and hauled to the picnic grounds. There we heard all the latest in music. In the afternoon several good readings were rendered. Then little Arden Kirkpatrick climbed upon a wagon and began as follows:

"When Pa is sick he almost dies.
He rolls his eyes and groans and cries,
'Send for Doc Brown, and pretty quick.'
When Pa is ill, he's a-w-f-u-l sick."

"That will be quite enough from you, Son: came his father's voice from the audience.

G.C. Worley, the clown and imitator of our Free West Society, mounted the platform and began:

"Ladies and gentlemen and fellow picnickers: When our worthy neighbor, R. V. King, first moved into our neighborhood, Mrs. Kendall sent her little son, Elton, down to see if they could assist them in any way. Upon his return, his mother asked, "What kind of looking neighbors are the new people?"

"Well," replied the son, "she looks all right, only ..."

"Only what?" prompted his mother.

"Well, as if she smelled something the cats had dragged in."

"And what does he look like?"

"Like what she smells," instantly replied the lad.

He talked on for half an hour or more amid continual uproar, telling something nice (?) on each family in our immediate neighborhood.

"Outrageous," I hear some exclaim. Not at all in the spirit in which it was given. Here it is only the spirit of the thing that counts.

Brownlow Humphrys, the good-looking brother of Mrs. Manford Flowers, was with us that summer, bringing with him his string instruments, including a bass fiddle. We were delighted to add him to our list of musicians.

During each summer, the people in what is called the "Rhodes' Settlement," some eight miles northwest, give a picnic. It is all prairie country. There we have tournament riding, broncbusting and goat roping. Such sports as I have not yet learned to enjoy. It is too dangerous.

Very often our relatives and friends from back east drive across state in their cars. R. T. Campbell, then a banker of Olney, Texas, and his family came one summer. Mrs. Campbell is the daughter of W. H. Keen. D. B. Koenand family of Wellington, Texas, also came in cars that summer. His two sons, Walter and Sammy, drove their two cars. W. T. Flowers and son, John, drove through from Denton, Texas, one summer in their Reo. John is now with the Fleischmann Yeast Company Shreveport, Louisiana. He was married a few months ago to a Waco, Texas girl, Miss Jewel Linders. Alton, our baby brother, is with the H. H. Harden Lumber Company, Waxahachie, Texas. There: I have mentioned each of my father's children, in case any of our many relatives, scattered over the U.S.A., may read these lines and know where each of us is living.

Our fourth year, Miss Rubie Mattingly from Lucy taught our little mountain school. That Christmas we had a lovely tree at the schoolhouse: also, an interesting program. Your scribe, dressed in a black grosgrain silk trimmed in jet, fashioned forty years ago, acted the part of an old maid in one of the plays. There were a few there who had attended the Christmas trees at Corona,

Cedarvale, Encino and Negra, and they said we had the loveliest tree and most interesting program they had witnessed. Quite a compliment for our little country school.

That was our last term in the mountains: the schools consolidated: all children now go in trucks to the Cedarvale High School. Mrs. H. S. Torrence (principal for the last five years and now engaged for the next) is the most beloved teacher by all pupils it has been my pleasure to meet. Miss Clara, her daughter, has assisted the past few years and will teach next term. She is still "Miss Clara" to the Primary grades, though she bears the dignified title of Mrs. J. H. Myers.

In the fall of 1920, our fourth year here, Cousin Adona H. Galbraith died. Her health had been failing for some time. While she was at the St. Joseph Hospital, Keokuk, Iowa, she wrote me and suggested, sometime during my leisure moments, to borrow some of the children's tablets and write a full account of all the happenings here, just as I had written them to her. She was sure it would prove interesting to many. My leisure moments are few, and I failed to comply with her request during her life, but have hoped for the time to come when I could. I never met her personally but once in life: I was then a child of seven. We have corresponded for years, ever since I was sixteen. She has always taken a great interest in my welfare. In fact, she has been a second mother to me, always remembering me with a letter and a little gift at Christmas and on my birthdays. As my cares grew heavier, her gifts became larger. At times when things looked discouraging to me, she would write encouraging letters, perhaps pointing out some way to make things more pleasant and reminding me "Into each life some rain must fall."

After she was too ill to write, her half-sister, Mrs. D. B. Ward (Cousin Ester as I call her, though we are no blood relation) kept me informed as to her condition, and, when she died, sent me Cousin Adona's personal things she wished me to have. Among them were her wedding silver, an amber necklace and one of her diamond rings. In her will she left me a few hundred dollars. She distributed her worldly possessions among quite a few, also to churches and cemeteries. How I have missed her dear letters, and how often my thoughts turned to her the past two years or more.

Eight miles east of us is the Marshall settlement. W. A. Marshall and family came before we arrived. They were stock men. Each son (six of them) who was of age filed on a section of land. They leased several sections and bought a few. The younger boys filed as they became of age. Mr. and Mrs. Marshall or "Daddy and Grandma Marshall," as they were called to designate them from their sons and wives, were as fine an old couple as I ever met. They were getting along in years but still young in heart and were ever ready and willing to assist in any improvement in our community. It was "Daddy" Marshall who took the lead in our singings or Bible Classes. It was he who dropped in at unexpected moments to cheer up a sick friend with his jolly and witty conversations. But a few months ago he was called to a higher mission, and our country has lost one of its finest citizens. All the boys are now married except two, Jurl and Tom, and we are listening for wedding bells over that way soon.

At the close of Miss Ruby Mattingly's school, we had our last entertainment at our little schoolhouse. Kenneth attended the Cedarvale school the latter part of the term that year and, at the close of the next term, received his eighth grade diploma. Not so bad after all for a boy taken from a good school, brought west to run wild.

That fall we made the best crops we had ever grown—feed, corn and cane to sell and twelve acres of our beans made one thousand pounds. They sold for $3.50 per hundred.

It isn't often you can hire help here, for each has all his own work to do. But during bean threshing, the men go from one place to another to help out. That means we "women folks" always have plenty of cooking to do. I, with my sister's assistance, have cooked all morning for a threshing crew for several days then stacked bean hulls or sewed sacks till time to prepare supper. J. L. Draper and I earned the title of champion bean hull stackers of our community. One afternoon I was on the stack when Mr. and Mrs. Kirkpatrick came by in their car. As they were leaving, Mr. Kirkpatrick said, "Mrs. Kendall, I want to get you to stack my hulls. You do the finest work of anyone I've seen."

Mrs. Kirkpatrick screamed above the roar of the thresher, "Mr. Kendall, I want you to come over and raise some good beans for me. You always raise the best crops in the country."

You see, we work but carry fun along with it.

About this time visions of a new house, a well of water on the homestead and additional wants began to rise on our horizon. No, we have no water, only dry holes: we have no machine in here to go through this rock. The R. V. King claim, joining us on the south, has a good well. Four miles north at the McDonald ranch is a fine well of water which waters hundreds of cattle and sheep. All in our settlement haul from these wells.

Our fifth crop was pretty fair. I can't remember just what beans brought that year, something near $4.00 per hundred, I think. We sold about one hundred fifty bushels of corn. Vegetables of most every kind do well here when there is season enough for the main crops.

Changes began to take place. Many, after securing deeds, moved away. The war claimed many young homesteaders, who never returned. Mr. Kirkpatrick and family moved away, waiting until their boys are old enough to help on the farm. Manford Flowers and family are also gone, and both families are now at Clovis, New Mexico. Eldgridge Flowers is there, too. Mr. Keen left for his Texas home. Fay, who is now Mrs. Stanley George, is with her husband in California, and "Billie" has wandered back to the old home. Miss May Cleveland and her mother, who lived near Cedarvale but came often to our gatherings, are gone. Miss Edith Mitchell, our trained nurse also of Cedarvale settlement but who visited us often, left on her usual trip a year or two ago, got married and forsook us entirely. Different doctors have located within twenty or twenty-five miles of us, one at Cedarvale, but did not tarry long. Each has passed on to other locations, leaving us as when we first came. Our only near physician is at Willard, twenty-two miles away.

One spring our sister-in-law, Mrs. Adron T. Flowers, took seriously ill. The nearest doctor was called and pronounced her case pneumonis and prepared to give her the serum, which she absolutely refused to take. He left the house, and Adron followed him to the car and asked him to leave her medicine of some sort. " It isn't any use," the doctor replied. "Wouldn't do her any good. She will be dead in a few days anyway."

Did we give up hope? Not at all. We wired our father at Denton, Texas, and her mother, Mrs. Mary Archer at Chillicothe, Texas, who came at once. Then we proceeded to doctor and nurse her ourselves. She is with us today, assisting the sick and needy who pass her way.

Last year, 1922, was our sixth crop here. The first of the year looked promising in every way. I, for one, began planning things. Allison, by baby girl, would enter school at the opening of the fall term, and I would be free during the day, as I had not been for twenty years. I gave my sons orders to quit riding Black Bess, my favorite saddle pony, as I wanted her for myself. How they laughed as they informed me I could not ride her for she would jump from under me before I got a mile from home. I promised to show them and smiled to myself. How strange it would seem to them to come in and call for me, as they always do on entering the house, to learn I was off for a gallop. But my glorious dreams lasted only a little while. A wireless message came informing me a little stranger would be with us in the fall. Well, anyway, I had a little bank account of my own: prospects for crops were good and we could manage nicely.

The thoughts of a new home and furniture also helped to lighten the burden. Then came the end of my dream although I did not know it at the time.

One year ago this month my husband was returning from Cedarvale when he was stricken down unconscious. We were expecting my father in from Denton, and all the relatives had gathered at our home to meet him. Mr. Kendall had told me he would be back at twelve o'clock. I waited until two o'clock then sent two of my boys to look for him, for I was sure something had happened. They found him at the house of our neighbor, Mr. Dexter Killingsworth, suffering death and still unconscious. Mr. Killingsworth was away, and only his wife and small children were at home. She had sent her little girl for a neighbor, Mr. Twyeffort, who went himself for the doctor, bringing him back in his car. This doctor did not even ease him, and as soon as I got to him had Dr. R. R. Davis of Corona called. He left with him at four o'clock for El Paso, Texas.

Mr. Kendall never regained consciousness until they reached El Paso. There he was examined in every way, X-ray pictures taken, everything they knew to do. Dr. C. P. Brown, head surgeon of the hospital, "Hotel Dieu," refused to operate because they could not locate the trouble. To make a long story short, he came home no better than when he left, only he was conscious. But his suffering was terrible. For months different doctors doctored him: hundreds of dollars had been spent for the restoration of his health. He is now at Lubbock, Texas, under a physician's care and has been for quite a while. He's slowly regaining his health. I have no idea how long we will have to keep him there. This doctor, M. T. Council, D. C., P.H. C. Chiropractor, says he has a tumor, the worst he ever handled.

On November 12, 1922, my little son was born. He was hearty and well until the day he was five months old, when he took laryngitis. Sickness again was abroad in our land. At every home near us one or more was ill. On that day our old friend and neighbor, J. L. Draper, was buried, having died with pneumonia after a Corona doctor attended him.

I walked the floor all night with my baby, with only my son to help care for him. Early next morning, I sent for my sister, Mrs. Koen, who had stayed with Mrs. Draper that night, and phoned Corona for our physician, Dr. Davis. He was away, but a new physician came and pronounced the case laryngitis and pneumonia in the right lung. We gave him medicine until midnight, but Roy Neil, my baby, grew continually worse. When we saw there was no chance for him, we put the doctor's medicine aside and doctored him ourselves. Oh, the agony of that moment when I had to take the whole responsibility on myself. The others (Mr. and Mrs. A. T. Flowers, Mrs. Koen and G. C. Worley) would not stop the doctor's medicine until I said to . Finally, I cried, " I risked it once before and saved a life, and I'll do it again." By morning he was better although twice that night they thought him dead. I had the doctor called again the next morning and told him I wanted him to doctor the pneumonia, but I would doctor the other if my baby went to choking again. He took it very well – said in such cases we had to try everything and keep trying. Roy Neil is still with us, healthy and happy.

A late drought cut last year's crop short, in fact, some made a complete failure. Our cane was fine, corn pretty fair but so little of it in the country the ravens wasted fully half of it. They came by the hundreds. We made one hundred and thirty-eight sacks of beans, got $8.50 per hundred, but it failed to pay all our indebtedness. Our relatives assisted us in every way possible, helping gather and haul off the bean crop. My father stayed with us until my husband returned from El Paso, Texas. Nell, my sister-in-law, did all my fall sewing and many other things. Nell often kept my two girls, Juanita and Allison, two weeks at a time, but, regardless of all that, I was almost run to death, very seldom getting a whole night's sleep.

In the fall Mr. Kendall's mother and only brother, John B., of Chillicothe, Texas, came and stayed two weeks. Our family and neighbors were kind and sympathetic, sending or bringing fresh fruit, vegetables, grape juice and other good foods.

Then came my illness, but I'll hasten over this as soon as possible, for I came nearer to death's door than ever before. Three weeks later, I arose from my bed, my strength and courage almost gone, and Christmas was drawing near.

On my birthday, the 13th of December, I was so tired and worn out and felt so miserable, I doubted if I'd ever live to see another. I rushed through with breakfast the best I could in order to have my children ready for the school truck. After I had finished my own breakfast, I was sitting alone at the table, wondering how I would make it through the day when Elton, my second son, came in and placed a box at my plate, saying, " A birthday present form Aunt Nell. I brought it home last night, but she told me not to let you see it till morning." It was a lovely tea-towel.

Ever since we came, I've always made little gifts for each child in our neighborhood each Christmas, but felt sure last Christmas was one time I would fail them. I was not able physically or financially. I tried to keep it from my mind, but a small voice kept whispering, "You know they will all be expecting their usual gifts from you." So with trembling fingers I went to work, fashioning lovely little gifts, also ordering quite a few inexpensive ones, doing without things I really needed to do so.

Just a day or two later came a letter from Mrs. D. B. Ward, Kansas City, Missouri, (the cousin Ester I mentioned) saying, with Christmas drawing near, she remembered how I always had gifts for the children, and she was sending me a little box for the neighborhood tree. Glad! Well, that letter contained all the Christmas gift I could have asked for myself! Next day the box arrived. Pretty trimmings for the tree which she knew we could not buy here: candy containers, chimes, handkerchiefs, books, dozens of pretty pins and cuff sets and lightweight candies to scatter among what she knew I would be making. Each child present and some who were not received one or more gifts from the box.

Soon came another box form our brother Eldridge in Clovis, dry goods for the relatives and a ten dollar check for the tree. Then another ten dollar check from John, our brother at Shreveport, Louisiana, with a short note, " I know it will not buy an automobile, but it will help decorate the tree." A few days later came another from Alton, our baby brother, and a letter explaining, "to buy candy, nuts and fruit for the tree." And when Old Santa arrived, I doubt seriously if happier youngsters could have been found anywhere.

Prospects for the 1923 crop can be told in a few words. Our late drought last year has lasted until today, July 7th, 1923. No crop to be made. People are leaving every day, driving their horses and cattle to the east until they find work. Soon there will be only a very few left, but, if any of you should pass this way, you will find me still on our claim. The life has been hard, my trials, at times, almost more than I could bear, and yet it has been a great pleasure, too. The future of our country has great possibilities and will advance by leaps and bounds when "moneyed men" turn their attention this way.

To our many friend and distant relatives, who have helped to brighten our sojourn here—by your cheery messages, subscriptions to magazines, seeds, flower plants and many little gifts—thank you. Though your name may not have been mentioned here, you are remembered in thought just the same. There have been many little incidents I would like to mention, but time forbids. My life is a very busy one, and there are only a few moments at a time I can "snatch" from my household chores.

Quite a few have come and filed since we came, but found the life so hard and moved on. Among them was my husband's only brother, John B. Kendall, who is now with his family in Kansas. Those who have left will someday wish they had remained. We have paid too great a price for this "free" land to give it up at this stage of the game. Happy? No, I haven't time to learn the meaning of happiness and will soon have less. My brother-in-law, G. C. Worley, and my "big boy," Kenneth, will leave for the east in a day or two, taking the stock with them. They will leave just what will have to be used on the farm.

My sister and five small children, one a baby girl who arrived just a short time ago, will stay with me. Elton, my second son, and I will have to do all the farming if any is done.

Contented? Yes, though I am left with my baby son in my arms, starvation apparently staring us in the face, my husband many, many miles away. But twice a week there comes a letter telling of his continued improvement, and the rest of my family as well.

July 7, 1923

Histories

The D. M. Allen Family

By Beatrice Allen Current

We, the Allen's, were living in Clovis, New Mexico. Mr. Allen worked in a grocery store for his brother-law, from 1928 through part of 1931. He came home one day and told Mother that there was a man in the store who said that he had a half-section of land with a two room house and a garage on it. He said there were over one hundred acres in cultivation and the main crop was Pinto Beans and some corn. There was no well.

Daddy said, What do you think, do you want to go out there? It is about four miles from Cedarvale and seven from Corona, and there is a school in both places." Mother asked, "How far is that from here?" (We had two Allen girls already married.)

Daddy said that Mr. Riley said it was about two hundred miles. That evening while eating our evening meal, Daddy told all of us five children and asked us one at a time to express our opinion. He said that there were mountains and the country was beautiful. One of my little sisters liked hot cakes so much, so she said, "Well, Daddy, we can eat bear and hotcakes." We never even tasted bear while there, let along have a diet of it.

We moved there the first week in February 1931. We, Mother, Melvin, Agnes, Wanda Lou and I, moved there weeks before Daddy and Margaret. They came through with our stock, feed and seed for the crops.

Melvin and I met some of the neighbors as we had to walk and carry water. They were very nice. Carroll, Jody and Doyle Berryman. We had the best crop that coming summer than we had ever expected. Our corn-crop had stalks that were twelve feet tall, and most had three or four ears on them.

We went to Singing Conventions on a school bus.

Mr. Ab Stroope was our first caller to welcome us.

We met so many nice people and we enjoyed school. We all worked hard on the place. We played the game of Forty-Two with different people.

Then came a drought and Daddy didn't put a plow into the ground. The next spring Margaret went to El Paso and worked in a factory. She met Roland Johnson and married him.

I met George Current and we had our first date June 15, 1934. We were married July 29, 1935. My parents and the younger ones moved to Artesia, N. M., and we later followed them there. My father died and was buried there in 1945. Mother died in 1974 at Wichita Falls, Texas.

The Armon Austin Family

Harvey J. and Roxie Austin, parents of Armon and Mozelle moved to New Mexico for Harvey's health in 1918 and filed on a homestead in Torrance County.

Armon was born at Lucy in 1918 and went to school there through the third grade. After that he went to Cedarvale to school through the tenth grade and then to Estancia to complete high school in 1938.

Ollie Steele was a student in Mountainair High School when they met. Her parents were Jim and Ollie Clark Steele. They had come to New Mexico from Texas and moved to a farm south of Mountainair. Jim Steele was originally from Tennessee.

Armon and Ollie farmed near Cedarvale until 1955. Then they moved to a home north of Estancia that was once called Witt. That was the location of the dry ice plant at one time.

The Austins had four children Bonnie Sue, Armon Lyndal, Neal Dwight, and Rollin Randolph. Neal Dwight died as the result of an automobile accident March 5, 1965, and Rollin Randolph died in Vietnam, May 27, 1968.

The mules that pulled a New Mexico covered wagon to Philadlphia for the bicentennial celebration in 1967 were raised by Armon.

While still retaining both homes, most of their time is spent on the ranch near Cedarvale.

Following: Taped interview with Armon Austin on August 6, 2007, at his home near Cedarvale, New Mexico, in cooperation with New Mexico Farm and Ranch Heritage Museum who transcribed this information.

ABSTRACT (Important Topics in Order of Appearance):

The tape begins with in the middle of a discussion regarding the federal government payments to farmers to not plant crops. Taped is turned off at consultant's request.

Interview session begins with family genealogy. Great-grandfather was born in Kentuckly and lived in East Texas before homesteading in Cedarvale, New Mexico. Armon's father was born in Leonard, Texas and was twenty-five years old when he arrived at Cedarvale. Originally his grandfather, father, and two uncles traveled to Cedarvale area in 1916 via Taos, N. M. They found a nice piece of land with a squatter's cabin on it. This 640 acres was purchased from the owner who lived in Lucy, New Mexico. Grandfather had to apply for the homestead rights. The family then returned to Texas, loaded up their household items, and transported them on the Santa Fe rail. The train route at that time was through Lucy, Willard, and then into Belen.

(More family history is reported) After the initial 640 acres was purchased, Armon's grandfather and sons homesteaded more property. In 1942, Armon bought 320 acres that his grandfather had homesteaded on. He shares the story of the time when he helped his father plow the fields. His father had traded a pair of binoculars for a gray horse, and Armon rode the sled pulled by the horse. He got tired of riding the sled ahead of his father so he wadded up the lines and rode on the horse. His father got him off the horse and back onto the sled, telling him that he would do a better job if he rode the sled. Armon did not see any difference, so he got back up on the horse. His father stopped him again and told him that the horse could throw him and then run over him with the "knifer"; he also commented that he did not have the money to buy a casket. Armon rode the sled until noon, and then rode the horse again. His father eventually sold the horse for ten dollars. The new owners of the horse got thrown when they tried to ride it. Armon's father explained that the horse had been a rodeo horse and would buck if it was saddled. The reason Armon did not get bucked off was because he had not used a saddle.

Armon describes the town of Lucy. It had a school, depot, blacksmith, justice of the peace, two stores, post office, and gas station. There was also a ladies' auxiliary there. Now the town of Lucy is mostly vacant homes. Armon was born in Lucy on a snowy night in February 1919. The doctor had come from Willard by train, and Armon's dad had sledded him to the house where Armon was born.

Armon remembers the drought in 1923 and recalls that people left the area to find work. Armon's family went to Clovis in search of work, while the grandparents stayed at the homestead. Armon's brother died in Clovis after being poisoned from tainted Vienna Sausages at the age of two. While the entire family ate the sausages, his brother had died after eating one bite. He is buried in Clovis.

The family lived in Clovis until 1928, when they returned to the Cedarvale area. They traveled in a Model T, pulling a trailer loaded with household goods. The roads were very treacherous, and climbing the Caprock of Post, Texas, was very steep and difficult. [Details regarding this trip are questioned, as Post, Texas, is not along the way from Clovis to Cedarvale.] Armon recalls that he and his mother were pushing the car up the hill when a man came along in a truck, offering to tow them up the hill. Armon was nine years old at the time. After their return to New Mexico, the family never left. In 1928, crops were just coming up when a hailstorm knocked the crop down. His father decided to stay in New Mexico.

Armon recalls that folks would go to Belen or the copper mines in Hurley in search of work during those drought years. There was a bumper crop in 1929.

The family grew corn, beans, and a little wheat. Beans were transported from Cedarvale to Duran by wagon and team. Armon recalls that his father sold his first crop of beans to a company in Duran.

Armon describes the family home. It consisted of two rooms: a 10' x 16' and a 16' x 16'. Water was hauled from the McGilroy Ranch. The family kept a barrel in the kitchen for drinking water; Armon recalls that it would freeze in the winter. Armon's father built a tank for hauling water and set it on the wagon. They dipped water into buckets and dumped the water into the haulin' tank. They had to pay for the water. Often his father would swap pasture grass to the seed man in exchange for water. The seed man was a sheep rancher and ran two bands of sheep (2500 sheep per band) on his land.

Armon recalls that they had milk cows. The family supported itself by selling corn and beans. He remembers that his mother put food up in canning jars. They raised hogs, and meat was often hung on the north side of the house or wrapped in a tarp. They raised chickens and traded eggs and cream for groceries. Staples of coffee, sugar, and flour were purchased. His mother would use fifty pounds of flour every three weeks. Armon comments that they got more bags back then than people get when they spend one hundred dollars today. He remembers his mother separated the milk and cream to churn into butter.

Armon says that farming is not work. He says it is just twenty-four hours a day steady. He has suffered health problems, but believes that God will take care of it. (The tape is turned off and restarted)

Armon tells the story of the time his father asked him to dig out a post that was in the field that was being plowed. Armon had not made much progress in the morning, so after lunch his father told him to take his water jar with him because he would not be returning to the house until the post was out. Armon says it did not take him long to dig up the post, since he did not want to stay out in the hot sun for long.

The consultant's mother had gallbladder problems; after Armon was born she needed to have surgery. She and Armon took the train to Woods County, Texas, where his uncle [mother's brother] lived. His mother had the surgery, and his aunt nursed him while his mother recovered. His aunt had a girl the same age as Armon, so she nursed them both.

Skimmed milk was often fed to calves once the cream had been taken off.

In the early years, Armon recalls that railroad workers would often throw coal off the train as it went by so that poor families could use it in the winter.

Prior to 1928, the family went to town by team and wagon, but that year his father purchased a Model T. In 1930 his father traded horses for a Garrett [unknown] car, which he had purchased in Albuquerque. Most trips to town were on Saturday, but they didn't go every week. When asked what they did for fun, he recalls that they had picnics, attended ice-cream socials or met for games. Often they would meet for singing conventions. These events were held at different houses throughout the area.

The local church, Center Valley Church, began as a community church. Several of the prominent families in the area were Baptist, so it eventually became a Baptist church.

The town of Progresso was the territorial capital of New Mexico [misstated: Progresso was the county seat for Torrance County from March 1903 to February 1905]. He says that in those days it seemed that the county seat was wherever the toughest people were. The interviewer recalls hearing a story that men from Estancia came to Progresso, removed all the records, and moved them to Estancia because they wanted it to be the county seat.

The railroad was taken out of service in the Estancia Valley area in 1930. Willard was the major stop for settlers arriving by train because they could get horses and wagons from the livery stables; they also could get the lumber and supplies that they needed. In the early years in the Estancia Valley, the grass was good and there were plenty of buffalo.

Armon comments that today "We're getting too sophisticated and educated to know your neighbors." (The tape is stopped and restarted) There is a very brief discussion of chivalry.

The consultant tells the story of his appendicitis attack, and immediate surgery in 1952 or 1953.

Armon tells the story of how he met his wife, their courtship, and their marriage. He recalls that her father wouldn't let them marry until she had finished school and had her diploma.

The consultant, his current wife, Margaret whom Armon married several years after his wife Ollie died (Margaret's husband had, also, passed away and she and Armon attended the same "Singings," which were events that the old timers traveled many miles to attend, they sang good old songs and enjoyed refreshments, usually once monthly) and the interviewer look at and talk about photographs of the old church and of baptisms held in water tanks.

Armon tells the story of the time he worked at the Estancia Hotel. After a run-in with a store owner about the return of an unused saw that had been purchased by the hotel owner, his father's advice was to not take anything from anyone. He had said, "If you don't go back to the store and whoop him, I'll whoop you."

The consultant continues the discussion of families in the neighborhood, and the names and location (east, west, south or north) of their land is given. The following family names are mentioned (in order):

Plant, Dominic, Gottley, Harris, Morris, Hawkins, Garret, Powers, Bayoff, Williams, Carella, Luna, Wright, Rhodes, Osborne, Harper, Brown, Mitchell, Maiz, Campbell, McCloud, Jones.

The Fred Belzer Family

By Evelyn Belzer Campbell

Fred Belzer arrived in Cedarvale in 1912 and homesteaded two miles west of town. He built a six room house with the help of neighbors, especially that of Dick Mitchell. In January of 1913 his family joined him, having come by train from Topeka, Kansas, to Torrance.

Fredrick's (Fred's) wife was Evalena Osmus before their marriage. Both were born in Iowa in the early 1880s. However, due to Fred's asthma his family moved to Colorado when Fred was seven years old.

On December 22, 1901, Fred and Evalina were married. To this couple was born Beulah on January 2, 1904, and Felma on June 3, 1905. A son, Frank Allen, was born in Topeka, Kansas, October 13, 1911. The Belzers had sold the Colorado farm.

Fred's asthma made it necessary to move again so at Mrs. Belzer's suggestion they moved to New Mexico. Fred farmed and also had a small grocery store in Cedarvale. As with most people of the community they milked cows and sold cream to a creamery in Trinidad, Colorado, when the train ran through Cedarvale.

The youngest daughter, Evelyn, was born at home by a Dr. Stone from Corona, on January 20, 1920.

Frank died in February of 1925 at the age of thirteen from uremia. Then in 1946 their home burned and everything was lost. They turned their milk house into a home with help from neighbors who made up $800.00 for them.

In 1949 Fred died in an Albuquerque hospital of heart failure. Mrs. Belzer lived until 1958 and both along with Frank are buried in the Cedarvale Cemetery.

Evelyn lives in Alamorgordo and attended the quilt show in Cedarvale of October 1988, winning a certificate of the most unusual quilt which she had designed, pieced and quilted herself.

New Mexico Farm and Ranch Heritage Museum, Oral History Program
Interview Abstract
Consultant: Evelyn Belzer Campbell, Date of Birth: 1920, Female, Date of interview: August 4, 2007.

The consultant was born three miles west of Cedarvale, N. M., in 1920. Her parents had come from Topeka, Kansas, to the area in 1912 to homestead. They arrived in Torrance, New Mexico, by train and traveled to Cedarvale by wagon.

Her father was asthmatic. His first trip to the Cedarvale area was with a friend. After three days of being able to breath better and sleep lying down, he was convinced that this was the place he should move to, so he filed a homestead claim. This homestead was 320 acres, or a half-section of land. He farmed pinto beans and feed corn. The beans were taken to warehouses in Cedarvale where they were cleaned and loaded onto the train for shipping after they were sold. Trucks were used for hauling after the railroad quit. Crops were fair and the prices were low in the early 1900s. Evelyn remembers that her father sold one hundred pounds of beans for fifty cents.

The family had cows, chickens, and horses. They sold cream for extra income. The consultant attended school at Cedarvale. She remembers that during the drought of 1926, the family moved to California for two years. She never finished school, only attending through the ninth grade. She was married at age fifteen.

Community families were involved in church, and Sundays were spent singing and visiting. After her marriage, her husband formed a baseball league. Her husband had come to New Mexico when he was four years old. The two met at school, and through parties, where they would dance, eat, and play games. She remembers the singing conventions that were held in the community.

She remembers that construction of the school began in 1916 and was completed in 1921. She discusses the layout of the school. At recess, the children played baseball and games such as Red Rover. She tells the story of the outhouse with the kissing hole. There was a knot in the wall of the outhouse, and the older students convinced her to kiss a boy through the hole. She was punished with no recess for three weeks and remembers that her mother was not happy with her.

She left the area in 1956. Her first child was born in 1938 in a dugout home.

Evelyn remembers the drought years, and that her husband sold their cattle. He went to work for Judge Hamilton in Albuquerque, and later moved to Alamogordo. Her mother stayed in Cedarvale. Evelyn got a job as a nurse's aide, but left after six months because the pay was not very good. Earlier in her life, she had taken the postal exam, but had not done anything with it. She applied for a job at the post office in Alamogordo and worked there for twenty-three years. She comments that the benefits are very good. Her husband died in 1999 and is buried in Alamogordo.

Doyle Berryman

By Doyle Berryman

Doyle Berryman came to Cedarvale in the spring of 1930 to help his brother with farming. The Berryman farm was three miles southeast of Cedarvale on what is now the Buddy Rose place.

Doyle's father had gotten this property in trade from Jake Richardson for his home near Robert Lee, Texas. Doyle lived on the Cedarvale property for five years.

In the early thirties, Sunday school and Church services were being conducted in the schoolhouse. Quite a large group of young people attended these services.

A minister by the name of Bob Smith came in 1932 from Littlefield, Texas, to help the Berryman's farm. Bob and Mrs. J. W. Donaldson began church services in that same year in the old Baptist Church that is now a barn belonging to Ramon Tenorio (1988).

Doyle's father and mother and their children moved to the farm in 1933. There was Mamie Ruth, Irene, Truitt, and J. G. coming later in the year.

Doyle recalls a revival held for a week in the summer of 1933, led by a cousin, Elmer Bird, in which twenty-five young people made a profession of their faith in Christ. That was a high point of Doyle's life.

Doyle and his wife Ina Bell make their home in Hobbs where they are active in church life yet.

The David B. Campbell Family

By Ruth Welch Campbell

The David B. Campbell family moved to Cedarvale in 1916 via covered wagon from Oklahoma.

At that time they had three children: Garvin, Lee and Roberta and another on the way. Don't you know that was a hard trip for Mrs. Campbell? They arrived in April and Nettie was born on June 14.

Mrs. Campbell was the former Ellen Draper. Her parents also came to Cedarvale and homesteaded. Mr. Draper is buried in the Cedarvale Cemetery.

Mr. Campbell homesteaded just north of the Pinos Mountains. He was a very successful farmer and was able to buy, for taxes, land that had been abandoned by less successful homesteaders thus accumulating enough land to have a nice sized farm and ranch, where he raised pinto beans and Hereford cattle.

Five more children were born into the family. They were David, Essie Mae, Lillie, Rosalie and Tolbert.

Mr. and Mrs. Campbell sold their place in the 1950s and moved to Truth or Consequences. Later they moved to Boonville, Arkansas. Mr. Campbell passed away in 1953 and Mrs. Campbell in 1972. Both are buried in Booneville.

At this writing all nine children are living.

The Candelaria Family

Juanita was born and raised in Cedarvale. She attended school in Cedarvale, Corona and graduated from Estancia High School. Her education was completed at New Mexico Highlands University. She taught school in Torrance County and she, also, taught in Paris, France, while Eleno was stationed there. When they moved to the old Candelaria place, Juanita went back to teaching school in the Mountainair School and retired in May 1973 with twenty years of service. She loves children and old folks.

While Eleno was stationed at Sandia Base, Juanita attended beauty school. She operated the Star Beauty Shop and the Mona Bella Beauty Shop which they still own.

Eleno retired in 1962 with twenty years of military service. In April 1965, Eleno and Juanita moved onto the old Candelaria place in Red Canyon and have remained there.

While Eleno, a native of Torrance County, was in the military during World War II, he served in North Africa and in Italy. He was hospitalized many times. His Army career took them to many states and many countries abroad including three years in Paris, France, where Eleno was assigned to Supreme Headquarters, Allied

Powers of Europe.

He served his last five years at Sandia Base in Albuquerque.

Eleno became interested in politics. He was elected Torrance County Commissioner four terms.

Juanita and Eleno have done a lot for the people of Manzano. For the past seven years, they have worked very hard for their Sr. Citizens Center. Much credit goes to Eleno and Juanita for making their Sr. Center what it is today.

The Earl Chandler Family

By Lavonia Chandler Wyatt

Earl and Maebelle Chandler and their family lived about six miles west and two miles south of Cedarvale, just north of the Frank DuBois Ranch. They lived there from February 1932 to August 1933.

They had two daughters, Lavonia, and Cleon. Lavonia was thirteen and Cleon was eleven. Two sons, Vermell and Dorvell age six completed the family.

Earl was a trucker and every Sunday morning as he drove the family to Sunday school and church in his truck, he stopped all along the way, picking up all who wanted to go along.

He served as Sunday school superintendent for the community Sunday school for a year. Maebelle was Sunday school teacher for the junior class.

Although we were only there one and one-half years we made many dear friends with whom we still keep in contact.

The Asa Cathey Family

By Owanda Cathey Keelin

Asa and Jewel Tombs Cathey came to New Mexico from Ryan, Oklahoma, in 1932. They lived on the Juan Gallegos ranch for two years and then moved to Cedarvale in 1934. In 1943 they moved to the Harry Smith place and stayed until 1943 when they moved to Santa Fe in December of that year.

Asa and Jewel had a daughter, Owanda (Sis) born April 3, 1925, in Fleetwood, Oklahoma, and one son, Dan, was also born in Fleetwood, October 29, 1923. Another son, Mike, was born in Mountainair, N. M. November 3, 1945.

Sis married Paul Keelin of Corona, N. M. in 1943 at Waurika, Oklahoma. All three of their daughters were born in Santa Fe. They are Janette Keelin Smith of Santa Fe, Danny Keelin of Durangeo, Colorado, and Kenny Keelin of Santa Fe. Sis has seven grandchildren.

The Thomas Colbaugh Family

By Rebecca Toombs Colbaugh

Rebecca Toombs Colbaugh was born August 10, 1924 in Fleetwood, Oklahoma, to George and Kittie Clyde Yates Toombs.

The family moved to Cedarvale in December of 1930. They lived in the old hotel until a house could be built on the farm.

Rebecca attended school in Cedarvale at the still standing school which was four rooms at the time. Some of Rebecca's teachers were Miss Jensen, Miss Dennis, Effie Harris, Mr. Twyefort and Gertrude Cobb.

After moving to the farm, Rebecca rode a school bus driven by Oliver Schneider. The bus was very old and very cold. Mrs. Schneider fixed a pipe through the center somehow, that kept the children's feet warm. Fred Lackey and Al Toombs also were bus drivers with Rebecca sometimes driving for Al while he farmed.

When in the eleventh grade Rebecca went to High School in Corona. It was there that she met Thomas Colbaugh. They were married February 10, 1943. For two years

Thomas was in the military service.

Their daughter, Karen, who was born March 28, 1946, was two months old when the family moved to Delta, Colorado, from Cedarvale. They still live in Delta.

The Elcie Currents

By George Current

We moved from Snyder Ranch near Snyder, Texas. Our family was Papa, Mama, Theo, Bee, Ima, and myself, George.

We first moved to Pinos Wells on a small place. I used a walking buster, and put up a lot of land. Then Papa found the place Mrs. Husband owned and we moved there into a brand new house.

As we were riding horses one day near a little house close to the road, my cousin told me that two pretty girls lived there. I told him that's where I aimed to start hitching my horse, in front of that house.

After awhile I went after water and one of the girls was at the windmill. She was so cute that I went home and told my mother that I had found my lifetime mate today! That was in January of 1934.

I took her to the mountains with Bee and his girlfriend, Paul Current and his girlfriend. We roasted marshmellows, and took pictures. We were ready to go down the mountain when I jumped and reached up for my girl and lifted her down through the top of a little tree.

I think that made an impression on her. That was June 15, 1935. We, Beatrice Allen and I have been married for fifty-three years. We have three wonderful children, fourteen grandchildren and eleven great-grands.

We lived for a year around Cedarvale after we were married and then moved to Artesia. We enjoyed living at Cedarvale and we went back a good deal for several years. We appreciate coming back now. My Parents, Theo, Ima and Lee are gone now. Ima's husband and son and Tena's husband have also passed away.

We still have fond memories of Cedarvale and Corona.

The Elmer W. and Cecil B. (Pyburn) DeVaney Family

Elmer was born in Yates Center, Kansas, in the same home his father was, on April 2, 1906. At age four and in 1910, he came with his folks to New Mexico on an immigrant train to Progresso where Pop DeVaney filed on his 320 acres and proved up on it. Elmer walked every day to school one and a quarter miles to the Sunflower School District 45, never tardy, and never finished high school.

In 1927 (spring) he rented land from B.E. Piggott and started on his own. In 1927, he filed for the last 320 acres homestead left in this community; and in January 1928 he built a log and proved up on his place. From this land he purchased more and more cattle which was his only source of income. Later on he had Bennie Maes help him make adobes and build on another room.

I, Cecil B. (Pyburn) DeVaney was born December 21, 1916, in Torrance Co., New Mexico, on my parents' Rennie C. and Alcy (Brown) Pyburn homestead west of Estancia. I lived in New Mexico all my life except one and a half years when the folks went to Ark by covered wagon and we came back in a Model T touring car. Being the oldest of four children I worked alongside my dad, and with joy. I listed with a six horse teams, cultivated, run a knife slide which my great grand-mother called a poor devil, helped haul logs from the Manzanos Mts. with team and wagons for our winter and summer use for we had cook stoves and heaters (wood burners).

I started to school at Ewing School with

Lola Dressler my first teacher and finished high school in Estancia with Miss Minne Laws the English teacher and principal of the school.

One of the most understanding teachers a pupil could have.

At a 4th of July celebration in Estancia in 1937 Elmer and I met. We went and had our picture made then to rodeo out to my home and had ice cream and cake. On 4th of Nov. 1937 we were married at my grandparents E.U. Brown. My mother fixed dinner and then we left for a short honeymoon trip to the Carlsbad Caverns. Came back to his or our home and finished the bean harvest.

In Aug. 1938 we were blessed with a baby girl Elsie Louise, Aug. 1940 Joyce Ann, 1941 Helen Fay, and 1943 a namesake Dick Edward, by this time our two room house, with running water, and 6 volt battery lights was too crowded. We went and got a permit from Uncle Sam, for all the materials were tied up for WWII. A contractor from Albuquerque, H.A. Hoach and his men started our new six-room with bath and basement when Dick was nine days old. We had a 32-volt wind charger, which were great lights until R.E.A. come in approximately 1953.

In 1947 Cleo May arrived and in 1949 our baby Fern Aline arrived forty-five minutes before Dr. Wiggons got there.

No PANIC Edna Gonce and Elmer did just great. Fern was her grandparents' (DeVaney's) golden wedding gift.

We are very grateful for all six of our children, fourteen grandchildren and three great-grandchildren. All six of our children and nine of the grandchildren are a child of God and work in his (Christ's) vineyard.

To this time July 29, 1980, the loss of our son-in-law Robert Haynes was our great tragedy.

The Elmer DeVaney Family

By Cecil DeVaney

Elmer was born in Yates Center, Kansas and at the age of four, he came to New Mexico on an immigrant train with his parents in 1910.

When he was twenty-two he homesteaded on the last 320 acres of land in this area. Having a saddle horse and a cow he called for a brand. He acquired the backward z and had it recorded for $1.50. Today it costs $50.00 just to keep it recorded.

Elmer and Cecil Pyburn were united in marriage November 4, 1937. They began their married life at Elmer's homestead which is the location of their home; this is twelve miles west of Cedarvale. All fifty years have been spent there. During those years they raised cattle and farmed.

All of the children, grandchildren and great grandchildren helped to celebrate their fiftieth wedding anniversary which was held in Cedarvale at the Senior Center.

The children are Elsie, Joyce, Helen, Fern, Cleo and Dick. Tragedy came in February, 1988 when the oldest, Elsie, was called home.

Cecil's hobby is piecing quilts and quilting. She has been active in the Cedarvale Quilting Club for forty-nine years.

Edna Dishman Tracey

By Edna Dishman Tracy

I was born October 14, 1898, at Blum, Texas, on a farm. My parents were Fraud and Hattie Dishman, my sister Lillie was born three years later. Early spring 1907, four covered wagons of us left Texas to homestead in New Mexico. My grandfather and grandmother Dishman, their two sons, Uncle Perry, Uncle Wilbur and Aunt Bessie, Grandpa had two wagons. Uncle Charles Knox and family, had a wagon and my folks one wagon. When we were six weeks from Texas to Willard, New Mexico, we were caught in two blizzards had to double up teams to get up some of the hills where the road was worse than cow trails, we were almost one day getting across seven miles of deep sands near Mescalero, had to let teams rest often.

One night we had no water for the teams; had to travel all day until after dark. When we came to a lake. The next morning there lay a dead cow in the lake. We had filled our water containers the night before we did not like Willard. We were routed by Corona to buy feed as there was none at Willard. We arrived Corona March 31, 1907, on Easter Sunday. There we homesteaded. I attended a country school called Varney.

My sister Mae, brothers Herman and Bud were born near Varney.

My husband's family came by train on February 14, 1915, from Chrystal Falls, Texas. Five years later, I was married to Raiford Tracey.

I had taught school at Varney and Gran Quirvera. Raiford and I had five children: Nell Ruth, Elvis, Glyn, Bobbie and Burnell.

We farmed near Corona until 1943. We moved to Oakland, California, where Raiford passed away in 1951. Bobbie and Burnell and I moved to Albuquerque 1953. Lived there for twenty years when Bobbie, David and I moved back near Corona.

I have twenty grandchildren and twenty-one great grandchildren and one on the way.

I like gardening, sewing and crocheting.

I've always loved people, church and I loved to go to school—every day.

The Foster Family

Lured by glowing reports of land to be had in the West two brothers, L.O. (Ottis) and W. E. (Edgar) Foster and Edgar's bride. Effie decided to come to the Estancia Valley. There to begin an adventure and a new means of making a living. At the time they were living in southern Missouri and northern Arkansas.

They left there by train in March 1908 and arrived at Willard, New Mexico, from where they looked over the surrounding area for a place to make a home. Edgar heard of plans to build a new town by the name of Cedarvale, twenty-five miles southeast of Willard and they decided to investigate.

Both filed on one hundred sixty acres near Cedarvale. Edgar was a carpenter and built one-room houses for them to live in. Life was not easy in the strange new land and hardships were many. Lack of water and dry years, perhaps the greatest. In order to have the land persons were required to live on it for seven months out of the year. Ottis worked away from his claim during the winter months in order to have some added income.

In September 1910, a daughter, Vera, was born to Edgar and Effie and then in December of 1911, Edgar died from typhoid fever.

Effie went to work at a hotel in Willard for a few months, but in order to keep her claim she returned to Cedarvale. She and Ottis then worked out a plan whereby he would do the farming and she the cooking, washing, cleaning, etc. for both homes. Later they decided to get married and did so in July of 1913.

Effie was the first schoolteacher in Cedarvale. She did not teach for very long. Through the years they added to their income by milking cows and selling cream, as well as chickens, butter, milk, and eggs, later selling the cows and getting range cattle in their place.

In 1922 a daughter, Helen, was born and in 1924 a son, Kenneth. Kenneth only lived until September 1928. Both Vera and

Helen received their grade school education in Cedarvale except that Helen attended the eighth grade in Corona. Vera graduated from high school in Estancia and Helen from Corona.

The Fosters were quite active in community affairs, especially Sunday school and church. Effie was a charter member of the Cedarvale Civic Club and helped in the quilting of many quilts. The making of quilts was her hobby. She also gave many hours of her time in caring for the sick in the community. Before the day when morticians became available she was called on numerous occasions to prepare a body for burial whenever a death occurred.

As time went on the Fosters gave up bean farming and relied on whiteface Hereford cattle for their income. Over the years, little by little, they added to the farm until they had four and one-half sections.

They lived at their home near Cedarvale until Effie's poor health caused them to live in Portales near their son-in-law and daughter, Helen, in 1962. L. O. died on August 12, 1971, and Effie on December 15, 1977. The daughters still own the land.

Vera was married to Sam Barnes and they had five children: Wesley, Phyllis, Sharon, Sandra and Larry. Helen married Dr. Floyd E. Toland and had one son, Lewis. Dr. Toland died in 1975 and in October of 1981, Helen married Tom Clark Livingston.

The Bennie Gallegos Family

Benjamin, (Bennie) is the son of Juan Gallegos and Concha Tenorio. Juan and Concha married in 1915 and they had eight children Ramona, David, Alfonso, Bennie, Patirico, Raynaldo, Emma, and Mike. Juan and Concha ranched in the Pino Wells area as did their parents.

Bennie attended grade school in Cedarvale and was graduated from Corona High School. After graduating he helped with ranch work, sheep and farming. In 1943 he joined the military service.

Corine Lucero Gallegos is the daughter of Refugio Lucero and Antonia Abeyta. She was born and lived in the Cedarvale area on a ranch her parents owned and operated with sheep and cattle.

She has a brother, Pete, and two sisters, Mary Ann, and Juanita. She attended school in Corona from first grade through high school, with the exception of a couple years after her father had died. After graduating from high school she worked for local merchants in Cedarvale for a year or so, then she moved to Vaughn. In Vaughn she went to work for the Citizens State Bank of Vaughn, where she worked for twelve years.

In 1946 Corine and Bennie were married. They went into business, owning and operating a gasoline station, parts house, and repair shop. Later they bought some land north of Vaughn.

They have three children: Jude, Inez, and Louisa. Jude is helping with the business in Vaughn, and is married to Diana Perez. Inez is a schoolteacher in Mountainair, New Mexico, and is married to Alan Carter. Louisa is a security guard at the World College of Montezuma in Las Vegas, New Mexico. One grandson, Matthew who after graduating from the Military Institute in Roswell, is presently attending college at New Mexico State University in Las Cruses.

Corine Lucero Gallegos

Spoke with Corine at her home in Vaughn, New Mexico, on the afternoon of March 28, 2008.

Born July 16, 1923, in Torin, New Mexico, at the home of her mother's mother. The doctor came from Corona to deliver her.

Corine's father and his three brothers were sheep ranchers between Cedarvale and Corona.

Corine went to the second and third grades at Cedarvale. There were approximately 100 students at that time.

Continued her education in Corona, New Mexico. Corine's father was a friend of Mr. DuBois in Corona who encouraged her father so send children to school at Corona. During Corine's high school days, her father rented a house in Corona from Mr. DuBois where Corine stayed while attending high school.

School buses consisting of a pick-up with a canopy on top and benches along the sides transported the children to school; first to Cedarvale and then to Corona.

Corines's folk's occupation was ranching. They grazed approximately 5,000 head of sheep and some cattle. Some beans, corn and hypar were planted. Ranchhands were employed to do most of the ranching and farming. Corine recalls that the farmhands ran the mule or horse teams to plow and to plant. Some forestland in the Gallinas Mts. was leased. Sometimes the family lived at the Rock House, which they had built at the Gallinas Mts. where a well was easily drilled and they raised a large garden including cabbage, "cucks," and many vegetables.

Corine's siblings include: Pete, now ninety-four and in a facility near Albuquerque; Quanita, eighty-eight retired school teacher; Mary Ann Tenorio (deceased) was a school teacher who taught at Cedarvale; Mary Ann and her husband, Ramon, and children still have property in Cedarvale.

Corine and Bennie Gallego's children are: Jude, who now owns and runs Phillips 66 station in Vaughn (previously owned and operated by Corine and Bennie); Inez, schoolteacher in Mountainaire.

Louisa Corine remembers that a shiny black automobile her father purchased had curtains.

Interviewer's comments:

Corine is a most lovely person and an excellent historian who lives with her husband, Bennie in Vaughn. Unlike many of the pioneers settling the New Mexico lands, Corine's family were already established there and seemed to been very successful. Apparently some of Corine's family has or had Spanish Land Grants around Belen.

The William and Cora Gladwell Family and Uncle Wade Gladwell

By Franklin Kimbel

They came to Corona on December 24, 1935. They had been picking cotton around Mangum and Altus, Oklahoma. Olen Shaw, a son of Cora Gladwell by an earlier marriage, brought them in a Model T Ford truck and returned to Oklahoma. This left them without transportation, very little money, and not eligible for relief because they had not been in New Mexico long enough.

The children were Beatrice, Charlie, Ollie, William and Clifford. They lived in the home of Mr. Dilbeck on the north side of Corona because it offered a chance for a better life.

The area around Wetumka, Oklahoma, was in a severe drought.

One thing they did have was a willingness to work. The children picked up split beans under the Corona Bean House. Uncle Wade worked wherever he could find a job. Their neighbors gave them a helping hand. To mention just a few, Noble Snodgrass allowed them to build a one-room shanty on the Snodgrass ranch, where they cut wood which was hauled to Corona and loaded on boxcars and shipped to woodyards. Charlie Vickrey provided transportation to the doctor. Frank DuBois looked the other way when they killed a deer. The Helen Foster family gave milk and other items.

The Gladwell family was living about five miles southwest of Cedarvale when Cora passed away on August 20, 1936. Will Gladwell was left with five children to take care of and provide for. Their ages were fifteen, thirteen, ten, eight, and four. By this time the family had been in New Mexico long enough to qualify for public work under the WPA Act.

Raymond Lackey loaned Will a wagon and team. He loaded, hauled, and spread caliche on the sandy road in Leonard Hobbs area. This was done with a pick and shovel. Will had worked in a coal mine so he was accustomed to hard work. He helped build the Cedarvale gymnasium. He walked about four miles to catch an open truck to work on Highway 60 in the Encino area. Will Gladwell passed away on November 4, 1937.

Olen Shaw came back and took the younger children to live with him in Bartlesfield, Oklahoma. Beatrice had married Raymond Lackey Sr. before her father's death and remained in the Cedarvale area.

Uncle Wade Gladwell was a strong believer in education. He encouraged Beatrice and Ollie to be more than uneducated housewives. He took care of a farm just as though it was his own. He would even put out fruit trees. He worked on a ranch owned by Frank DuBois. When his brother died, Wade went to his daughter's near Steamboat Springs, Colorado.

All the Gladwell boys served in the Army, including their half-brother Olen Shaw, except William, who was in the Merchant Marines.

New Mexico proved to really be a land of opportunity. Ollie returned and lived with Raymond and Beatrice and Grandma Ethel Lackey. Later, Clifford came back to Raymond's and Beatrice's.

All the Gladwells now live in New Mexico. Beatrice married Franklin Kimbel in 1953 and lived in Belen until her death on June 14, 1987. She had two children, Wanda Mae Lackey Wood and Raymond Lackey Jr. Charlie lives in Peralta, just south of Albuquerque. He is married to Bonnie Proctor, from the Elvy Proctor family of Cedarvale. He had two children by an earlier marriage, Allen Gladwell (deceased) and Judy Gladwell Huckaba.

Ollie married Jake Honeycutt of Corona. They live in Ojo Caliente in Northern New Mexico. Their children are Jake, Kenny, and Larry.

William married Bonnie Wilson of Bartlesville, Oklahoma. They have two homes and live either in Belen or Truth or Consequence. They have two boys, Paul and Eddie.

Clifford is married to Linda Wood, a sister to Bill Wood, who married Wanda Lackey. They live in Espanola and have four children; Leslie, Brenda Gladwell Dye, Mike, and Scott.

I was warned to make clear the following comments are my own. All the Gladwell men have worked one or two jobs at a time and lots of overtime. The girls have kept house, reared families and worked in the public a major part of the time. They are a close-knit family and help one another. They are energetic, conscientious and help the needy. I think one of the reasons is because of their early hardships and the example of the Cedarvale people.

The Charlie Gonce Family

(Written by Edna Wright Gonce at separate times)

Charlie Gonce came to the Progresso neighborhood in 1930 from Mineral Wells, Texas, to work in the bean harvest. Edna Wright had come from west Texas at the age of five with her parents and had been living in New Mexico since then.

Charlie and Edna met and were married

on February 1, 1931.

I, Edna Irene Wright Gonce, was born in Dawson Co., Texas, January 18, 1911. My parents, Mr. and Mrs. William M. Wright, nine brothers, two sisters, and myself came to New Mexico by covered wagon driving our stock in the fall of 1916. We rented the Metcalf place, where we farmed until Dad filed on land and we had our own home.

My dad and mother belonged to the Primitive Baptist Church and my dad preached part time.

I went to school at Progresso and Cedarvale.

Charlie Gonce came from Mineral Wells, Texas, in 1930 to sharecrop with Fat Elliston. We met and were later married on February 1, 1932. To our union was born a daughter, Charlotte Mae, and six years later a son, William Leonard. Our daughter married Nathan Strong, they had two sons. Nathan passed away in 1969. Our son married Judy (Hodgin) and they have two children, a daughter and a son.

We share cropped with Mr. Jockey for two years, then rented the Beedle place for about three years. We then worked for Mrs. Osborne for about one and a half years. In 1938 and 1939, we rented the Jockey place again. In 1940 and 1941, we rented the Bob Elliston Place, while there, we bought land and built our home on it; where we are still living.

Leonard and his wife Judy bought his father's ranch and live about one mile from Charlie and Edna who remain on the home place. Charlotte Gonce Strong lives in Albuquerque.

Our family all are members of the Southern Baptist Church. We have four grandchildren and three great grandchildren.

The "Red" Goodwin Family

By Violet Goodwin Lucero

Redden and Addie Pennington Goodwin left the dust bowl of Oklahoma in 1932, and moved to Cedarvale, N. Mex. They arrived, in a covered truck, at the George Toombs Ranch, with five daughters, Jewel, Opal, Lomita, Violet, Betty, and a married daughter, Willie Faye a.k.a. Billie or Bill, her husband, Dick Martin, and a German shepard dog, along with all their possessions. And another daughter, Gladys, and her husband, Jack Weathersby, followed them, several years later.

George and Kit Toombs had been friends, and neighbors, in Oklahoma, their daughter, Lois, had married Addie's nephew, Cad Stiggins. Therefore, they already knew people in the community.

The Goodwin family rented a farm from Refugio Lucero, and moved into what was known as the "Rock House" they lived there for many years. Some said the house was haunted, and it appeared to be, for some strange, and unexplained, noises were heard, not only by the Goodwins, but by visitors, also.

The girls attended Cedarvale, and Corona schools.

Redden, Addie, Billie, Gladys, Jewel, and Lomita, are deceased. Opal lives in Peralta, N. Mex. Violet in Rio Rancho, N. Mex., and Betty in Lewisville, Texas.

The Thomas A. Gregory Family

By Ruth Lackey Husband

Mr. and Mrs. Thomas Allen Gregory came form Hico, Texas, to Cedarvale in 1916. They filed homestead papers on a place one and one-half miles southeast of town. The papers were filed August 14, 1916.

T. A. Gregory was born at Cain Hill, Arkansas, November 18, 1859 and passed away March 17, 1945. His wife, Belle Gray was born at Troy, Texas, October 5, 1865, and passed away December 16, 1954.

T. A. Gregory was a cotton farmer in Hico, Texas, and when he came to Cedarvale he grew beans and corn. They came from Texas on the railroad and had their personal belongings and some animals shipped with them. He farmed until 1934 at age seventy-five. He didn't have any tractor so he followed his mules as he farmed.

The Gregory's were blessed with three children; John, who remained in the Texas area, Oscar (George) who came to Cedarvale and married Blanch Lively and had a family of four. Their one daughter, Anna Belle was a schoolteacher and she married Roy Vaughn whom she later divorced. Then she married Thomas Husband who was from Wales. They had one child, Thomas This son married a Cedarvale girl, Ruth Lackey, and they have four children; Thomas, Ray, Beverly and David, all living in California.

The Gregorys were an asset to the Cedarvale Community. They hired some of the local boys to help farm which helped them financially.

Everyone loved the Gregorys and they were missed when they left the area.

The Beryl Gustin Family

By Beryl Gustin

Herbert and Lua Staley came to New Mexico in 1911 from Kansas and filed on a claim at the south end of the Mesa at Progresso. Mr. Staley worked as a machinist in the railroad roundhouse at Estancia.

In December of 1911, Glen Gustin came to New Mexico and married Clara Staley, a daughter of Herbert Staley. They returned to Progresso and filed on a claim in the Snake Hills where he began farming and ranching. In 1943 he sold his land and moved to Colorado Springs, working there for one year. Then Glen and Clara returned to Estancia where he farmed, ranched and moved houses. He retired there but later he moved to Truth or Consequences, New Mexico.

Beryl, the youngest son, was born at Progresso in January of 1922. He attended the first year of school at Lucy, the second year at Cedarvale, the third through the eighth at Willard and High School at Albuquerque High.

On August 4, 1942, Beryl was married to Dorothy Toombs, daughter of W.L. (Dub) and Elsie Toombs, of Cedarvale. Four sons were born to Beryl and Dorothy. Larry and family and Ronnie and family live at Mountainair. Daryl and family live at Portales and Terry and family live at Belen. There are nine grandchildren.

Beryl joined the U.S. Navy in October of 1942 where he remained for over three years. He was stationed in Norman, Oklahoma; San Diego, California, and Seattle and Whiskey Island, Washington. He trained for aviation metalsmith and welder.

While stationed in San Diego, Larry was born in the hospital on North Island. The other three boys were all born in New Mexico.

April of 1945, Beryl boarded the aircraft carrier U.S.S. *Ticonderoga* and spent six long months on it in the Pacific Ocean around Tokyo Bay.

He was honorably discharged from the service in November of 1945. He and his family moved to Portales and farmed for one year. Then they moved to the Estancia Valley where Beryl farmed and ran a dairy. This they did until December of 1961 when Texas began to ship milk to New Mexico and there was a surplus. Thousands of gallons of milk had to be thrown on the ground as the milk plants wouldn't buy it.

The cows were sold to Bernie Wallace and Beryl went to work in January of 1962 for the New Mexico Department of Game and Fish. They then moved to Las Vegas, New Mexico, and farmed for the department. He farmed for it for fifteen years. After that they moved to Artesia to farm grain for the wildlife. He retired in 1986.

The Arthur R. Hamilton Family

By Paul Hamilton

In 1922, along with his father, John Ellis Hamilton, Jr., and their families, Arthur and his wife, Lucy; with their children: Nellie; Maude Paul; and Mabel, left the lower Rio Grande Valley, in south Texas, to settle in Torrance County, New Mexico.

Arthur "Buck" and Lucy homesteaded on a section of land about a mile and a half northwest of Torrance. Their first home was a dugout. The upper portion was constructed with railroad ties. It made a very cozy home for their growing family. It was snug and warm in the winter, and cool in the summer.

Unfortunately, during the next three years there was a drought that forced most of the farmers to go away each winter to work, in order to survive. Arthur and his family went to Roswell for two seasons, returning each spring to the homestead. The third year he worked for a while for the railroad. When that job ended, they went to Hatch, New Mexico, and later to Safford, Arizona, where they picked cotton until the picking season ended. Again they returned to the homestead. After that year the rains came, again, to the Estancia Valley and they were able to stay on their farm.

Arthur leased another half-section and during the following years farmed, raised cattle, and drove a school bus first to Cedarvale, then to Corona. The children attended the two schools in that same order.

During this same time, Arthur did some well drilling and put in a bean re-cleaning business in Cedarvale. He first bought beans for the Jensen Bean Co., then for Trinidad, Colorado Bean Co. and later became an independent buyer.

During these years their family had grown. J.W.; Mary Margaret, James, Rosalie and Jack were born in New Mexico. Nellie married Jesse Small, Maude married Wilsie Rinker, Paul married Joveta Ingraham, Mable married Eddie Weiderman, J.W. married Ernestine Armijo, James married Sue Bradley, Mary Margaret married Rudy Tyson, Rosalie married James Holman and Jack married Louise Robbins.

Arthur loved baseball and boxing. For a number of years he served as manager and member of the Cedarvale Baseball Team. He also enjoyed sparring with our local boxer, Pete McCloud, and helping him with his boxing career. Lucy kept busy with her family and her church. However, she was never so busy that she could not come to the aid of anyone who needed help.

The three older boys were in the service during World War II. Paul was in the Air Force; J.W. and James were in the Army.

Lucy passed away in 1941. It was a sad time for her family. Jack was only seven years old. Later, Arthur sold the farm. He moved to Truth or Consequences, New Mexico. Jack and Rosalie grew up there and Arthur remained there the rest of his life. He died in 1975 and is buried in Corona, beside Lucy.

Nellie died in 1965. Maude now lived in Texas. Paul, J.W. and Rosalie live in New Mexico. Mabel, Mary Margaret, James and Jack are in California.

The John Ellis Hamilton, Jr. Family

By May Hamilton McCredie

John Ellis and Maggie May Hamilton arrived in Torrance County, New Mexico, in 1922, with their four children. Maye was seven, William was five, Fannie Lee was three and John was almost a year old. We had moved from Hidalgo County, in the lower Rio Grande Valley of Texas. Along with us were Dad's father, John Ellis Hamilton, Sr., his stepmother, Mary Ann, and his teenage sister and brother, Ann and Walter; and his brother Arthur, and his family.

Dad met a man named Alfred Gunn who wanted to sell his interest in a half-section, two miles east of Cedarvale. Dad bought it and the claim was transferred into his name. Three years later, he received the Patent Deed. Grandpa Hamilton filed on a half-section about a mile southeast of Pinos Mountain, and Uncle Arthur and Aunt Lucy settled about a mile and one-half northwest of Torrance.

During the next three years not enough rain fell to raise a crop, so each fall and winter our families had to go away to work. James Robert, "J.R." was born in Dexter in 1923, Judge Thomas in Lake Arthur in 1924 and Rosemary in Salem, in 1926. Our mother died three weeks after Rosemary's birth and about five weeks later, baby Rosemary died, too. Not until I became an adult, could I really appreciate what our father had gone through. He never complained, just continued to do his best to take cake of us. How fortunate we were to have him for a father!

In April 1927, while on our way back to the homestead, we lost our grandmother Hamilton. She was killed in a wagon accident on the summit of the Organ Mountains, east of Las Cruces. After her death Grandpa made his home with us.

This left Dad and Grandpa with a farm and six children from one and one-half to eleven years old. Maye, being the oldest inherited the task of taking care of Judge and J.R. who could not care for themselves. There was also as much of the housework as she could handle. William helped Dad with the farming and other outdoor chores. Fannie Lee and John were in between, able to care for themselves but not big.

We farmed the homestead in 1927. The drought had broken and we never failed to make a crop after that. Dad, eventually bought an adjoining section of land and throughout the years he farmed, drove a school bus for a couple of years, threshed beans, and raised cattle.

In the meantime we children grew up. I married Jack Parker. We had five children: Jean, Jo Ann, Carole, Robert W. "Bob", and Vivian.

William married Violet Goodwin. They had two children: Sandra and John. Fannie Lee married Bruce Milton. They had three daughters: Beverly, Linda, and Cathy.

John joined the Army and was a prisoner of the Japanese for about three and one-half years. After returning home, he married Genevieve Chandler. They had three children: Cheryl K, a baby boy who did not live, and Joni C.

J.R. also served in the Army. He married Betty Goodwin (sister to Violet). They had five children: James R. "Ray", Terral "Terry", Patricia "Patty", and twins, Donald and Betty Jo.

Judge married Odessa Dunn. They had four children: Ronald "Ronny", Tommy, who died while still a baby, Mary Ann, and Stephen "Steve". Judge too, served in the Army.

Grandpa Hamilton passed away in 1940 at the age of eighty-three. He was a wonderful person, always cheerful, kind and considerate. How we missed him! He is buried at Cedarvale.

In 1956 or 1957 it was discovered that Dad had cancer. He sold the farm to Steve Pounds, who still lives on it, along with his wife, Myla. They raised their sons there. We love to visit the old home place. Steve, Myla, and the boys make us welcome.

My husband, Jack Parker, died in 1961 in California from a heart attack. Our brother, J.R. also died from a heart attack in 1978 in El Paso, Texas.

At the present time, September 9, 1989,

Fannie Lee (divorced form Bruce) and her second husband, Ray Sharkey, live in California. William (divorced from Violet) and his wife, Lillian, John and Genevieve, and Judge and Odessa, live in New Mexico and I divorced from my second husband, Walter H McCredie, live in Paso Robles, California.

Judge Hamilton

New Mexico Farm And Ranch, Heritage Museum Oral History Program, Interview Abstract
Consultant, Judge Hamilton
Date of Birth, October 22, 1924. Gender: Male
Date of Interview: August 4, 2007

The Cedarvale area began planning for a reunion in 1982. Prior to 1982, families would camp in RVs at the schoolhouse.The idea to have a reunion was brought forward. The first reunion was held in 1983 with 350 people in attendance. The reunion has been held every two years since that time.

The consultant was born in Lake Arthur, N.M [1924]. His father had begun farming at Cedarvale, but drought forced him to look for work in Lake Arthur until he could make enough money to plant another crop in Cedarvale.

His father had purchased the homestead in 1922. In 1926 the family had not made any money, so the family moved to Las Cruces until enough money could be made to return to farming in Cedarvale. That year, the consultant's mother died, and one year later, his dad and the six children returned to Cedarvale. On the return trip over the Organ Mountains, Judge's grandmother was killed when the horses bolted, overturning the wagon. Judge's father took her body to Salem and buried her beside his wife. His father was able to make a crop and stayed in Cedarvale. In total the family held 960 acres of land. The consultant's father later remarried; however, that marriage only lasted for three months. When Judge was sixteen years old, his father married again.

Judge recalls that all of the children had chores to do, such as dishes, washing, and ironing clothes. When the family returned to Cedarvale in 1927, Judge would go to school with his sister. His father had kept his sister out of school for two years to look after Judge, and the school finally told him that she should return to school and bring Judge with her. Judge was four years old at the time. In 1928 he fell at school and broke his arm. It did not set properly, and has been crooked ever since. He does not recall what he did while he was at school with his sister.

He attended the Cedarvale School through ninth grade, and then went to school at Corona, but attended only a few months before quitting. He says, "I knew more than the teacher did." He served in the military for two years, then returned to the farm "to get rich." In 1946 or '47, he recalls that he planted eleven sacks of beans and harvested only nine, and realized he would not get as rich as he thought he would. He left for Albuquerque and worked as an apprentice carpenter. He worked for the same company for twenty-six years and served as general superintendent for the last fifteen years he worked. He retired at age fifty-two in 1976 and lived in Arizona for eight years. His wife died in Albuquerque in 1994. He now lives in Truth or Consequences. He recalls the burning of the Harper Store in Cedarvale in 1940, which was never rebuilt, and remembers that in 1942 all the young men went to war.

W. T. Hesters

by Pallie Hester Dishman

The W.T. Hesters spent a few years after their marriage living on small farms along the state line dividing Georgia and Alabama. On March 16, 1892, their first child was born, she was named Zelpha Palestine. When Pallie, as she has always been known, was nine years old the family moved to Texas settling in the Ft. Worth area. Seven other children were born to this family with the oldest daughter taking much responsibility with the younger ones. As was true in most families in those days, the children all helped work in the fields as soon as they were old enough to chop cotton, or pick cotton, or whatever the chore might be. Schoolhouses were some distance from home and the children walked the few miles everyday carrying a lunch in a small tin bucket, or other container.

When Pallie was seventeen she married her childhood sweetheart, Wilbur Dishman, who had come to Corona in 1907, along with other members of his family. The wedding was in Wienert, Texas, and the date was September 12, 1909, her first trip to Corona was on the train as a young bride. Wilbur had a job in a general mercantile store in Corona where they lived until they decided to prove up on a homestead a short distance north east of town. They built a four-room house and lived there for some years while he continued with his job at the store. When their daughter was nearing school age they moved to Corona and have continued living there.

From the beginning Pallie seemed to have a talent for doing for others, helping wherever help was needed. During the Flu epidemic in 1918 she and her husband spent many nights sitting up with desperately sick people. She made burial garments, comforted the grieving and helped in many other ways.

Through the years her artistic talents seemed to come through and she has spent many hours with her hobbies, making gifts for family, friends and for visitors who happen along to see her crafts. One of her special joys is the Cedarvale Quilting Club to which she has belonged for more than fifty years.

As the years have gone by she continues to be interested in community activities, church, hobbies and especially in people. Nothing thrills her more than to have someone stop in for a little visit. Truly her house is the House By the Side of the Road.

Daniel T. Hileman Family

Daniel T. Hileman and Margaret Ann Purdue Hileman came to Cedarvale before 1909. The exact date is unknown. They left Cedarvale about 1918 and moved to Oklahoma. Margaret died there in 1918 and Daniel in 1922. While in Cedarvale they bought the hotel which had three rooms to rent. Mrs. Hileman did all the cooking and served it family style.

Only two of their five children came to Cedarvale. Robert Dell married Edith Bell Tonkinson, daughter of Matthew Peter and Carrie Louise Tonkinson, on November 28, 1911. Nine children were born. The first six children were born in Cedarvale. Twin boys were born dead on August 15, 1912.

Alice Irene Hileman Ward was born June 14, 1913. Homer Alva, April 10, 1915, and died October 24, 1929. Della Louise Hileman Lisk was born October 20, 1916. Ruth Elizabeth Hileman La Prade was born May 24, 1920, and died April 1, 1985, in Sumner, Oklahoma. Isabel Margaret Hileman Teague was born November 19, 1922.

Robert Ben Hileman was a bean farmer and homesteader until 1918 when he returned to Oklahoma,.where he became a mechanic. He bought the first car in Cedarvale in 1917. He bought a gas station, garage and blacksmith shop.

After a time he had to sell his business because of his health. Tuberculosis was contracted following the flu and he returned to Cedarvale and its dry climate. He lived outdoors the first three weeks and had to rest and eat properly. Smoke from his blacksmith shop and the mechanical work had aggravated his condition. Little rest and much stress also were contributing factors.

The second stay at Cedarvale was from 1922 to 1924. He left again, but this time he went to Vaughn to be a mechanic there. In 1928 he moved to Santa Rita, New Mexico, where there was open pit mining. After retiring he lived in Silver City until his death in 1967.

Gladys Cawer Keelin

Corona New Mexico
September 24–80

The history of Gladys Cawer Keelin age seventy-nine. I started this journey May 18, 1902. Borned to the home of Andrew Jackson Cawer and Stella Maude (Horn) Cawer at Paris, Texas. I had an older sister and two years later another sister was born. My mother passed away at this time and my baby sister Opal, my sister Beatrice and I lived with our grandparents as our dad went to the Indian nation and farmed. He sold his crop and came home but he had been gone long enough that Bea and I had forgotten him. He bought us a Big Doll and we wanted it so bad but we wrapped grandmother Horn's big gathered skirt around us with only our faces showing but with persuasion we did except the Dolls. I was four at that time. Dad remarried and I was so pleased to have a new mama. We then moved to New Mexico came to Melrose but it was winter and very cold and mama was having a difficult pregnancy so the covered wagon was hard on every one "but" we had spent a lot of time in it. It was comfortable but crowded.

We had a little Batcholer heater with oven and it seems like we always had cookies often.

Wondered how mama managed.

When we decided to go back to Texas. We went back to Paris and lived there and close by until I was ten years old. By that time we had three more sisters and later a brother, Frank, and another sister. "At" age sixteen, I married William Thomas Keelin (Bill) his home was at Honey Grove, Texas. He was born there and lived around Honey Grove until the year we married then we moved to Savoy where our first son, Jon was born then later we had three more sons Paul, David, Alvie, and two daughters Peggy, and Anita, we moved to Corona, New Mexico, February 22, in 1935 and have made our home here by since. At times Bill worked at Holloman Air Base in Alamogodo, and he worked for the R.E.A. when it came to Corona, and sometimes with the state, and county in roadwork.

I'm so happy that we are having a senior citizen place at Cedarvale and I'm sure I will enjoy it.

Sincerely Gladys Cawer Keelin

Paul Lackey Family

By Grace H. Lackey
Looking Back

My parents, Mr. and Mrs. John Humphries grew up in Kentucky, married and moved to Kansas, they ran a hotel and farmed. Their home was blessed with three children Alma, Iva and Roy, then mama lost her health, the doctor recommended a high dry climate. Papa came to New Mexico in 1909, it was still a territory. He filed on a claim then went back to Kansas.

In August 1910 he moved his family to New Mexico by train. The neighbors were at the depot in Progresso to meet them with wagons and moved them to the homestead, about two and a half miles south of Progresso and they put up a large tent and fixed a bed so my sick mother could rest. In the fresh air and sunshine she soon recovered and lived seventeen years.

In 1913 they lost a baby girl Malinda, hers was the first grave in the Humphries Cemetery.

They didn't get water on that side of the claim so they drilled a well on the other side, got water and moved over there. Then I arrived on the scene October 25, 1916.

More people had moved into the community by that time so they built a log schoolhouse in the center of the community—all the men helping. This little schoolhouse was the gathering place for all the people, in this happy thriving community, we had school, school programs, church, singing conventions, box suppers, and even Spanish classes.

One of my childhood memories is the New Mexico central train that ran every day, two miles north of my home, we could hear the whistle and see it flying along bringing mail and supplies from the outside would. At that time Progresso was a nice little village.

The winter of 1918–1919 there was a very bad snowstorm, the snow was so deep the train stalled on the track. I could see the men working all around it. It was loaded with feed for the ranchers hungry cattle, I remember papa and the other children had to wrap up and cut soap weed for the cattle until they could get the grain.

It was lonesome not to see the train when the track was taken up in 1929–30.

Paul's parents Mr. and Mrs. W. D. Lackey were married in Texas. They had three sons, Raymond, Fred and Paul. Mr. Lackey lost his health, so they decided to move to New Mexico. They left from Robert Lee, Texas, August 12, 1916, traveled in a covered wagon twenty-one days, September 1, 1916, they arrived in Corona, New Mexico. Mr. Lackey filed on a claim near Cedarvale, where they lived until the bad winter of 1918–1919, he said he wasn't a prairie dog, so they bought a place up close to the Gallinas Mountains, which now belongs to the sons.

Paul grew up roaming the hills with his dogs, helping on the farm and attending school in Cedarvale and Corona, he graduated from high school and took one year of business school in Abilene, Texas. He returned home, bought some land and cleared the timber and made fields. The summer of 1934 was so dry he went to Estancia and got a job working in an abstract office for Mr. Hall, he worked several months before returning to his place.

The summer of 1929 Mrs. B. E. Piggoit brought her four daughters and baby son to spend the summer with us. The youngest daughter had had a very bad case of pneumonia and needed our hot New Mexico sunshine and fresh air. So we had a happy time working and playing. When the crops were lean and laid by for harvest time, papa took us to the mountains for an outing. In those days mountain climbing was one of the main sports. And who should arrive on the scene but the Lackey brothers to climb the mountain with us. My brother had given them an invitation the day before when we had arrived and made camp for the night. That's when I first met Paul, our friendship continued, grew into a courtship, and after I graduated in May, from high school at Willard. We were married November 4, 1934.

The first year of our marriage we share cropped with papa in the Progresso Community. In the fall our first son was born. Wesley David the first grandson on either side of the family. After the crops were all harvested we moved to our own place near the Gallinas Mountains where we still live.

Our home was blessed with five more little boys, John Archie in 1938, Paul Daniel in 1941, Norman Joseph in 1943, Roland Keith in 1945 and James William in 1948.

Then the dry years started in. We couldn't raise crops so Paul would work on carpenter jobs, he worked on the construction of the houses at the gas plant below Corona, and the gas plant close to Mountainair, and on school houses in Durango, Colo., Albuquerque, Alamogordo and Carrizozo. He also worked on some highway construction jobs putting in bridges etc.

The boys and I stayed home and held down the ranch, took care of grandmother Ethel and the boys attended school, Paul came home on weekends to be with us and take us all to church.

The boys all grew up, graduated from high school at Corona and got their college degrees in the University of New Mexico.

After the nest was empty Paul and I built cabinets for several years beside taking care of grandmother Ethel, our cattle, and raising a garden.

All our boys are married, at last we have our daughters. We have ten grandsons, nine granddaughters and one great grandson.

Wesley is pastor of the Bethany Presbyterian Church in Dallas, Texas. His family is grown, two of them married, they all live in Texas.

Archie works at Sandia Corporation in Albuquerque. He is a computer technician he and his wife and his family live at Tijeras, New Mexico.

Daniel and his wife and family live in Farmington. He is a math teacher in the Bloomfield schools.

Norman and his wife are missionaries. He and his family are in Puerto Rico.

Roland, his wife and family live in Cuba, New Mexico. He is head of the science department and teaches physics, chemistry and science.

James and his wife and family live at Aztec, New Mexico. He is a math teacher. They all own their own homes and they and their wives are active in the Lord's work, for which we are very thankful.

Proverbs 22:6, "Bring up a child in the way he should go and when he is old he will not depart from it."

The W. D. Lackey Family

By Fred Lackey

William David and Ethel Lackey and their three sons, Willie Raymond, Fred Henry and Paul Joseph arrived in Cedarvale in 1916 from San Angelo, Texas. They came by covered wagon with the chuck box on the back. The lid of the chuck box made their table. They were able to have fresh meat all the way and the lakes were full of water. Mrs. Lackey would cook sour dough biscuits in a Dutch oven. As they traveled across the prairies they used cow chips for fuel.

The first of September, Mr. Lackey filed on 320 acres of land. Cedarvale had a railroad then. Mr. Lackey had lumber for their house shipped here from Willard which he used to build their home.

People were filing all around Cedarvale, then fencing their land and building homes. Cedarvale was lively then with two churches, the Nazarene and the Baptist; two stores and the post office.

At one time there were three warehouses all full of pinto beans, even beans stacked outside, covered with tarps. Beans was the money crop but cane and corn were raised for livestock. Hogs were raised for meat and lard. Milk cows provided milk and butter. There were also some range cows.

Nearly everyone has left and the ones

who were here in the early days and are still around have retired. Cedarvale no longer has a store or post office.

Mr. Lackey died in 1934 and Mrs. Lackey in 1974. A younger brother has also passed away.

Fred and Elizabeth Marable Lackey are the only ones of the family left at Cedarvale.

Cad C. Livingston Family

By Jack Livingston

Cad Livingston, his wife Inez, and son Tom Clark, came to Cedarvale from Hamilton, Texas, in 1921. Tom Clark was just short of four years old when they arrived. They came by train and shipped livestock and household goods by boxcar. Cad and Inez bought land about three and one-half miles southwest of Cedarvale. They had two additional surviving children, Leslie Reps (Jack) born in 1923 and Inez Lucille (Babe) born in 1927. Another son died as an infant.

Tom Clark, Jack and Babe all went through grade school in Cedarvale and then graduated from high school in Corona.

The Everett H. "Pete" McCloud Family

By Pauline McCloud

Pete moved to Cedarvale from Big Spring, Texas, where he was born and lived until he was eighteen years old. He lived with his grandparents, Mr. and Mrs. C. L. Fletcher. He worked for them until he joined the CCC's . He stayed in that work until it was disbanded.

He boxed during his younger years, being up for the state championship when he took pneumonias which almost ended his boxing career. Later he did have a few bouts locally.

He was employed for most of his life as a state highway employee and retired from that in 1974. He had worked some at ranching, blacksmithing and farming. He passed away in May of 1980.

Pete and Pauline Smith were married in February of 1938. She has lived in and around Cedarvale all of her life. She attended Cedarvale School until her senior year when she went to Estancia.

To this couple were born six children, five girls and one boy. They are Nora Ann, Mildred, Gayle, Bonnie, Shirley, and Leroy.

Up until 1952, Pauline had been a homemaker but at this time she became postmistress, a position she held until 1988 when the post office was closed.

She was also grand chief of New Mexico for the fraternal Order of Pythian Sisters. She is a lifelong member of the Cedarvale Quilting Club and still resides in Cedarvale at the site of the first post office building in Cedarvale.

I Pauline McCloud, was born to William C. and Nora Smith near Cedarvale, N. Mexico. Living the first six years of my life eight miles west of Cedarvale on homestead of my father's, now owned by Leonard Hobbs. I attended my first year of school from there, but for some reason the bus wasn't going to go by the place, so consequently we moved on my grandfathers place just two miles from Cedarvale where I lived the rest of my single life.

In 1932 I met Pete McCloud who moved here from Big Springs, Texas, in order to help his grandparents farm, milk cows and raise sheep. On February 23, 1938, we were united in marriage.

Our first child was born January 25, 1938, a girl Nova Ann, second girl Mildred Faye, November 22, 1941, third girl, Maraguerite Gayle, May 3, 1944, fourth girl, Bonnie Belle, June 29, 1946, first and only boy Lester Leroy, September 1, 1947, fifth girl Shirley Mae, December 21, 1949.

We built and lived in a half dug-out the first year of our marriage, farming one of my father's fields also helping Mr. McCloud farm.

In 1940, we moved to the Clint Smith place, my father's dad, farming it until 1945, Pete took a job working on the Highway 54, near Corona, and we moved to Cedarvale. When the job was finished he went to work for Soil Conservatories, when they had funds, until 1952. While not working for SCS during this time he had a blacksmith shop, also, worked on various farm and ranches.

In 1952 he went to work for Torrance County, as blade man, until January 1959. At that time he went to work for State Highway Department, continuing to work for them until his retirement October 1976.

In 1947 our home burned to the ground and we were unable to save anything. With help of our neighbors and friends one month later we purchased and moved into another home, during the month we were living with my parents.

In 1951 we took over a grocery store from Pete's father, he retired, later in July of same year I was appointed postmaster, in 1966 we moved the post office into a room adjoining our home, closing store, and as of this writing I'm still postmaster. Pete passed away May 15, 1980. I'm still living in our home and proud grandmother of sixteen grandchildren.

The Jack Mitchell Family

By Lois Mitchell Graham

Jack and Hettie Mitchell moved to Cedarvale in January of 1913. Clint and Rosa Smith had moved to Cedarvale from Missouri a few years before; Rosa was a niece of Jack.

Clint went back to Topeka, Kansas, and Missouri on a visit and while there he talked to the Mitchell's about filing on a homestead in New Mexico. In 1912, Jack, his nephew Dick Mitchell, and a neighbor, Fred Belzer, made a trip to New Mexico to see the country. They each filed a claim for a homestead before returning to Topeka.

Each one had to build a house on their land. So during the summer of 1912 they built homes. Jack Mitchell chose a place just a quarter of a mile west of town and Dick and Fred Belzer's places were three miles on west.

After the houses were built the three men returned to Topeka and in January they chartered a freight car and moved all three families with their furniture to Torrance. From Torrance the furniture was hauled to the home sites at Cedarvale by team and wagon.

The Mitchell family had seven children. One was already married and remained in Topeka. Clarence, Fred, Hazel, Neil, Dorothy and Lois made the trip to New Mexico. They lived in a little two-room house until spring, and then Jack bought a two-story house from someone who had already given up and left. Jack had this house moved to his place. The house had a large living room, a large kitchen and three bedrooms.

At that time Cedarvale had one grocery store, the post office and a few homes. Mrs. DeWolf was the postmistress and Mr. DeWolf did some farming. There were very few families in the area when the Mitchells arrived. The L. O. Fosters, the Smiths, the Tonkinsons and a Mr. and Mrs. Shipp and their family were there. A few families lived toward the Gallinas Mountains.

The schoolhouse was four and one-half miles southwest of Cedarvale and church services were held along with a Christmas program. Everyone went because it was the only thing in the way of entertainment.

Soon other people started moving to Cedarvale and before long there were box suppers and parties. Mrs. Lola McCanna, her brother George Lee, and his son Ralph, lived toward the Gallinas. They had a large house and an enormous living room, so they began having dances.

By this time families had moved to the area and other buildings were put up in town, including another store.

The Lively family and the Waltons had places east of town. The Livelys had three grown daughters and they organized a Literary Society for entertainment. The school was moved to Cedarvale and church services were held in it.

There were no conveniences. Wood was hauled from the mountains and water from the Belzer place. He had drilled a well. The Mitchells had three big water barrels to haul water in. A team of horses and a wagon was used to haul the water.

Jack had to work away from home most of the time in order to make a living for the family. He was a brick and stonemason. He and Mr. Matt took a tract to build the schoolhouse in Cedarvale about 1917.

Wood was the fuel used for cook stoves and heaters. Rainwater was caught when possible to wash one's hair because most well water was too hard.

In the early days there were no regular ministers but different pastors came off and on from Estancia or Willard or maybe Corona. At other times there was Sunday school and someone would talk and there would be singing.

About the year of 1916 the Graham family came from Texas and bought a place just a short distance north of Cedarvale. Mr. Graham was a Baptist minister and preached there for quite awhile.

Lois Mitchell, daughter of Clarence Mitchell married Mark Graham, son of the minister, Graham. She and Mark went back to Topeka, Kansas, in 1919.

Hazel Mitchell was a sister of Lois Mitchell Graham and she married P.L. Mitchell who was no relation. Tom Pounds bought P.L.'s place in 1950.

Lois Graham has three children: Dale W., Mrs. Lorraine Dalrumple and Mrs. LaVerne Nelson.

The Boyd Moseley Family

By Bill Moseley

Boyd and May Meyers Moseley came from Benjamin, Texas, to Cedarvale in a covered wagon. It was in Novermber of 1911. With their eight-month-old Bill, they first lived in an old house about two miles southeast of Cedarvale called the Burchfield place.

In early 1912 they homesteaded on land about seven miles southwest of Cedarvale. There was a house built there as well as times would afford, with lumber hauled from a mill near the mountains. In those days the neighbors were good to help each other to get started.

Land was cleared of cedars to farm and to raise a few cattle. Water had to be hauled by team and wagon from nearby wells for a long time. Later on more land was rented and bought.

The neighbors all got together and built a country schoolhouse where all the children went to school until later on they were bussed to Cedarvale.

In February of 1915 another son, Charles, was born into the Moseley family and then in December of 1916 a daughter, Dorothy, was born. The family lived around Cedarvale until the late thirties.

Bill and Charles went to Yuma, Arizona, where Bill went into the grocery business with his uncle. Charles worked as a carpenter. He married there and reared a family. He remained there until his death in July of 1977.

Dorothy went to El Paso, Texas, in 1938

to attend nursing school at Hotel Diue. She was employed later at William Beaumont Army Hospital and from which she retired in 1981. She still lives in El Paso. She had married Jack Kiely in 1941. He died in 1977. They had one son, Jackie, who now lives in California.

Bill went to El Paso in 1943 where he was employed in the post office. He married his wife, Lorene, a nurse at Providence Hospital. They retired a few years ago and still live in El Paso.

Boyd and May moved to El Paso in 1950 and lived there the rest of their lives.

Of all the hard times and good times and ups and downs, "mostly downs" they enjoyed Cedarvale, for the Lord was with them all the way. Quote, "As I see it."

Maxine Pounds Brown

New Mexico, Farm and Ranch Heritage Museum, Oral History Program; Interview Abstract
Consultant: Maxine Pounds Brown
Date of Birth: August 24, 1928
Gender: Female
Date of Interview: August 4, 2007

The consultant's father came from Kansas and met and married her mother when she was sixteen years old. She was from the Pinos Mountain area of New Mexico. Her grandfather, E.E. Pounds, originally purchased land and sold a half-section to her father. She recalls that her grandfather had wanted to be a cowboy at age thirty-four.

Maxine was born in an adobe home in 1928. The home had once been a stage stop. The home and one-and-a-half sections of land were purchased from a Mexican man and was located five miles from Cedarvale. Her parents eventually built another house. Maxine's father ran sheep and cattle on the land. She says that she was her dad's "boy." In 1934 her dad sold the sheep because her mother hated them. She has two siblings, a younger brother and a sister.

Maxine attended the Cedarvale school, which was a one-room school house. After one year, a larger school had been built, and she attended it until she started eighth grade. After eighth grade she attended the school in Corona.

She married James Brown in 1954 and now lives on the old Gustin place. Her husband received a GI loan for $10,000. He paid $9,600 for the one and a half sections and ran cattle on the land. Maxine grew up on horseback, and recalls that there were not many social events with the neighbors. Wagons were used for travel. She says that she was scared on her first day of school and remembers that the vehicle was not a real school bus as we know it today.

Her father was hard on her and gave her many chores, including caring for the cows and chickens. The family made income from trade for fruit; she says that it was hard work to put up the produce in jars. Her father was not happy with her when she decided to go to school in Las Cruces for two years. She eventually went to Santa Fe and found work in a bank. Her father wanted her closer to home, so he got her a job at the Corona Trading Company as a bookkeeper until she married.

The tape is turned off while they break for lunch. After lunch, the discussion is centered around Maxine's children and the death of her son.

John W. Richardson and Family

Background

My heritage contains no one of great fame, however I am proud of the driving pioneer spirit which has predominated in both paternal and maternal families. This spirit was based on religion, patriotism, and a strong desire for freedom of enterprise which allowed me to be born and raised at Cedarvale, New Mexico, in its very early days shortly after New Mexico was granted statehood.

My mother's family, the Waltons, after fighting in the Revolutionary War migrated from Virginia, through Kentucky, Missouri, Texas and then to New Mexico. They were religious, of Scotch-Irish-Dutch descent, wealthy and definitely pioneers. My father's family, the Richardsons, migrated after the Revolutionary War from Georgia, through Tennessee, Arkansas, Texas, to New Mexico. They were of English-Scotch-Irish descent and were also pioneers.

The Walton Family

My great grandfather, Jacob C. Walton, whom I knew for a short time, was born on a large estate in St. Louis, Mo. In 1836 his father, Judge Thomas G. Walton, was killed while protecting his family and home from renegades after the Civil War. His mother, Susan Harden Stith Walton, was left with a large family and an estate which was finally confiscated by high taxes in 1877. At that time J. C. Walton brought his wife, Luisa Jane (Shannon) Walton (who was an accomplished musician) his children, his mother, feather beds, and an expensive parlor organ to Texas. He set up a trading post on the Ailene, Kansas, cattle trail near Santa Anna, Texas.

My grandfather, Hugh W. Walton, born in 1859 in Missouri, helped construct the trading post and rode the cattle trail until his marriage to Nora Hasty in 1884. He settled in Brown Co., Texas, became a farmer with cotton gin, and raised two boys and four girls. One of the girls, my mother, Anne Myrtle Walton, was born in 1894. She was taught music by her grandmother and became well known for her talent on the organ and piano. She met my father at an "All day singing and dinner on the ground" affair.

The Richardson Family

Records of the Richardson family date back to 1779 in Georgia, where Joel Richardson owned a slave or two. It appears that his son Ben Richardson was born in Tennessee. Records show that Terrel Richardson was a son of Ben Richardson and was born in Tennessee. Terrel moved to Ozark, Arkansas, where my grandfather, John F. Richardson was born in 1843. My grandfather moved to Llano Co., Texas, and married Victoria Mitchell in 1873. He moved to Coke Co., Texas, bought a small farm, raised four boys and four girls, and became a Primitive Baptist preacher where he was well known and loved as "Uncle John" throughout Texas. He was the pastor of a small church for many years. One of his boys, Marlin Jacob Richardson, was born in 1884, became an entertainer of a sort with excellent talent on the mandolin, Spanish guitar, and voice. He was very much interested in the lady with such talent on the piano.

My parents were married in 1912, the year New Mexico became a state. They were in Texas at that time but the lure of free land and enterprise brought them and the Walton family to Cedarvale, New Mexico, shortly after my sister, Nora B. (Richardson) Wyatt, was born in 1913.

My grandfather Walton sold his cotton gin in Texas and bought two sections of land about four miles southeast of Cedarvale where he built a house, barns, fences, blacksmith shop, and drilled a very productive well nearby. He is said to have built or helped to build the existing Cedarvale schoolhouse. Hugh Walton got a list of the names of all the children of school age, made a trip to Santa Fe, and induced the state to build a school.

My Aunt Rosa (Walton Lackey) and her family rented a place on the northern edge of town. My uncle Creight Walton bought property about a mile north of town. The rest of the family, Aunt Ruth, Aunt Bertha, Uncle Bill, Uncle Martin lived on my grandfather's place for a short while.

I am told that I was born in a half-dugout on my grandfather's place on April 3, 1916, becoming an early native of Cedarvale. No doctor is listed on my delayed birth certificate. However, Mrs. L. O. Foster, a good friend of the family signed the document which later became very important to me.

Life was a little raw in the early days of my life. We moved frequently to find work. My father taught school at Cedarvale for one year, moved to Texas for a short time, then to Mesa, Arizona, where my brother William Boone was born in 1919.

My mother and three children moved back to the homestead at Cedarvale while my father worked in the copper mines in Arizona for two years. We survived in a small one-room shack without water, fuel, telephone, or transportation except for two horses and a wagon, but we had good neighbors, good relatives, Mr. Harper's general store, and Mrs. DeWolf's corn mill.

In 1921 my father returned in time to see our homestead shack burn to the ground. This traumatic event was softened greatly by the kindness of the people at Cedarvale. We had a new house in about a week and all the furnishings required for survival given us as well as the feeling that the community was one big family and we were a part of it.

In 1922, my father taught school at Gran Quivira, N. M. As a beginner I advanced rather rapidly under his constant tutoring. I was in the fourth grade by the end of the year.

We hand planted, cultivated, and harvested about one acre of pinto beans in 1924, bought equipment, fenced the homestead, drilled a well and started farming in earnest in 1925. We expanded our farming and ranching in 1926 by purchasing the "Lee" place, a section of land near Refugio Lucero's ranch southeast of Cedarvale.

Two important events happened that year. I acquired a horse of my own, Bald Hornet, and a baby sister, Dora Marie. Of course the new sister was much more important to me than the horse, however I surely thought a lot of that horse, for he gave me another degree of freedom. I was completely satisfied with the way things were going.

All good things must come to an end, and in 1930 my father, over strong objections from the children, traded properties and half of the mineral rights with Mr. John G. Berryman at Robert Lee, Texas. We moved there in the late fall. We hired a cowboy to drive sixteen head of horses through, which took about two months.

I finished my last year of high school and college in Texas and started an engineering career in San Antonia, Texas, in 1937. In 1940, rumors of romance and high pay in aircraft design at Los Angeles, California, lured me there where I was fortunate enough to do some design work on the PT-13 trainers with Vultee Aircraft. I was transferred to Nashville, Tennessee, in 1941 to help design dive bombers. It was there that I met a young lady, Ella B. Benton, who was on a college ballet dance team, had a nice family, and was related to Thomas Hart Benton, the senator who had dueled with Andrew Jackson. In 1942 I was transferred back to Los Angeles to help design the first jet aircraft which was quite a breakthrough in aircraft propulsion.

Miss Benton and I kept a fairly healthy correspondence going by mail and in 1943 we were married at the "WeeKirk O the

Heather" in Burbank, California. In 1946, we were blessed with a baby girl, Barbra Joan, but saddened by the death of my mother, who had been in ill health for some time. I had joined the Army in 1945 and was with the 2nd Army Headquarters in Baltimore, Md., when my mother died.

In 1947, I obtained a design position with North American Aviation Co. and helped to produce on of their best fighter planes, the F-86, which was used in the Korean War and by military demonstration teams throughout the country. After our second daughter, Judith Diane, was born in 1950, we started migrating back to Tennessee by doing consulting work with various aircraft companies in Dallas, Fort Worth, St. Louis, and Akron, Ohio.

By 1958, we had settled in Nashville, Tennessee, with a home and a design job at Arnold Engineering and Development Center where I found ground test facility design for space vehicles very challenging and interesting. We created the environments for testing all military and some of the NASA space vehicles, including simulation of the sun, the absolute zero temperatures of outer space, zero gravity, and hypersonic velocities. Our home life was brightened in 1961 with the birth of a daughter, Jane Carole. In 1965, my father died with a stroke shortly after finishing a sermon as guest preacher in Oklahoma.

I obtained an M. S. degree in engineering science in 1973 from the University of Tennessee and advanced to supervisor of mechanical design at AEDC in 1979. In 1984, I retired and opened an engineering and consulting business in a building we own on Nashville's Music Row.

SYNOPSIS

My life has spanned some of the most significant events and developments in all history. I have survived two major world wars and a traumatic Depression. I only hope that my contributions to this world have helped in the advancement of human comforts and in the preservation of human freedom.

I have been fortunate in being a part of successful development teams but my early days at Cedarvale, New Mexico, seem more meaningful than mechanical achievement. The barefoot trips of exploration, horseback riding in races down the steep slopes of the Gallinas mountains, fall harvests, pie suppers, Spanish, and many other events that were a great joy to me. I am happy to have been free to walk the way the wind blows in New Mexico.

T. M. Richardson Family

By Jack Livingston

Tom M. Richardson, his wife and two sons, Guy P. and R. Ross came to Cedarvlae from Hamilton, Texas, by covered wagon in 1917. Guy was sixteen and Ross was fourteen years old at the time.

A married daughter, Inez, remained in Texas with her husband, Cad C. Livingston until 1921. The Richardson's bought land two miles west of Cedarvale and lived there until 1944.

Guy Richardson married Nettie Campbell, a Cedarvale girl. They had two sons, Marvin and Bill. Guy and his family moved to Arkansas about 1950.

Ross Richardson went to Colorado when he was about twenty years old. He married and lived in Colorado for most of the remainder of his life. He and his wife, Leona, had one daughter, Leona Inez. (Peggy).

Edna Robinson

Corona and Cedarvale, New Mexico
February 15, 1982

A transformed Texan, I am proud to call New Mexico my home—my roots have been set deep into this "land of enchantment." Though, memories of a happy childhood and early years of my life are reflections too.

I was born at Ingram, Kerr County, Texas, in 1908 at the home of my great grandmother, eleven miles from the home on a goat ranch where I was to spend my growing up days.

I attended a little country school built on our place in time for my first year. I was the oldest child so had no one to lead the way. My graduation year was spent at Trinity High School, Kerrville, Texas, eighteen miles to go in a Model T car and a brother to drive. That was the closest affiliated high school this was quite an adventure into the "Big World" for me but also a great experience.

Still young, my parents were not ready for me to leave home, so I spent another year at our newly consolidated school at Hunt, Texas. I took first and second years Spanish that I would need for college, a county extension field course in agriculture for interest and fun, played basketball and had time for many activities including school plays, this I call my "fun school year."

Then, still loving school, I persuaded my parents to let me go to San Marcos, Texas, to a teachers college. Still eighteen when I got my certificate, I taught my first school in Bandera County, Texas, adjoining Kerr County and not too far from home. The next four years I taught in my home school at Hunt.

In meantime while teaching, I attended summer school in summers at San Marcos and Alpine, Texas.

At Alpine I met my husband to be, Elvin Robinson. We were married August 27, 1932, at Roswell, New Mexico, on our way to a claim I had filed for a homestead that joined land my father had bought in Torrance Co. between Corona and Duran, New Mexico, this is where we started our married life. That and some more land we acquired, comprises the small ranch that we still live on today here we have spent most of our fifty years this coming July together.

After we married we built a "half dugout" adjoining a small two-room frame house my family had helped to build on the claim that's where our first child, Lyndon, was born in 1935. Also the year my father, Cleveland Griffen died.

In 1938 we went back to Texas to help my mother during the illness and death of my grandmother who lived with her. There our son Derrell was born in 1938 and my mother came to live with us.

In December 1939 our daughter, JoAnn was born. Rex was born in 1944 and another son, Keith was born in 1947 who passed away in 1975, the victim of cerebal palsy.

Having been close home for almost twenty-eight years I needed people and I found them in the quilting club at Cedarvale where they quilt, visit, eat good country cooking and enjoy country living to the fullest. The club merged with senior citizens for that was what we had come to be. We are fond of our center and for those who made it so—all of us together.

Signed, Edna Robinson

Marie Zelpha Robinson

September 1980

I Marie Z. Robinson was born February 27, 1910, on the Sand Hill Ranch near Kermit, Texas, that my father owned, to parents Homer and Elizabeth Jackson. My father was born March 2, 1883, in Jack county, Texas. My mother was born in Sullavan, Missouri, November 28, 1882. My parents sister Connie Laurie, brothers C. H. and Clyde, and myself came to New Mexico in June 1917 in a car, shipped our household goods and stock by train.

My father filed on a place at Gran Quivira, N. Mex. We lived there two or three years then my father bought the Mc Donald Ranch about one and a half miles from our homestead and I lived there 'til I married. I met my husband Loy A. Robinson at his father's store in G. Q. in 1920. His father J. J. Robinson was born April 22, 1862, in Greenville, Louisiana. His mother Dora Lee Robinson was born April 2, 1870, in Nevada, Texas.

Loy was born April 23, 1910, at Pyke, Texas. He had five sisters and six brothers.

Loy and I were married on February 27, 1928, in Carrizozo, N. Mex, Had seven children five girls, Corine, Lorine, Joann, Shirley and Annie. Shirley passed away at two years old. Had two boys Delbert and Jerry. We lived at or near G. Q. till we moved to Wash. State in 1945 stayed there two years. My husband worked in the Puget Sound Navy Yards. We moved back to G. Q. and stayed till about 1950 and then went to Albuquerque, N. Mex., where we stayed till my husband retired from Sandia Base. We moved to Cedarvale in 1973 where we live now.

Oliver and Jettie Schneider

By Sibyl Schneider Brown

Pioneers of Cedarvale, New Mexico

Homestead location: Approximately thirteen miles NE of Cedarvale, or five miles SE of Pinos Wells

Children:

Bayne, married Chester Black—Rt. L, 2203 W. Berrendo, Roswell, NM 88201

Oliver, Merchant Marine, Died World War II, on SS American Leader ship September 10, 1942

Sibyl, married "Wee" Griffin, after his death, married James Brown, 1977- Luna Rt., Box 301—Reserve, NM 87830.

In the spring of 1929 the family sold a small dairy farm in Mississippi, near Biloxi, having an adventurous spirit, and hearing of the land available under the homestead act, started west. This trip was made in a Model T Ford with their four children.

After five day's travel we arrived in Clovis, where we stayed and worked for a short time, inquiring about the country further west. After moving on to Roswell and Mescalero inquiring there about homestead land, it was decided Mountainair would be a good location.

On our way to Mountainair via Corona, we had a flat tire as we came over the mountain to Cedarvale. Those were the days when you stopped and fixed the flat. During this course of action Mr. John Hamilton came by on his way to Cedarvale. He stopped to offer help, and during this time he inquired as to where the Schneider family was headed. When he was told, Mountainair and that we were interested in homestead land, he assured us that if we didn't' find what we wanted over there, he could help us locate something at Cedarvale.

After spending the night in Mountainair, it seemed Cedarvale was calling so we went back. With the help of Mr. Hamilton the site was located, and paperwork was completed to move onto the homestead.

The recent abandonment of the railroad between Torrance and Willard, via Cedarvale, made crossties available, as the tracts had been removed. These ties were used for the outer walls for the first two rooms of the homestead house, where later a side room was added, with a "half dugout" to the back side. This was a time when everyone worked together, families and neighbors as well. When something needed to be done in a short time, all the neighbors helped.

This was a special time as the children played games, rode horses without saddles and sometimes made the trip to the nearby "Salt Lakes" where wild horses ran in herds.

Dry land gardens and crops of pinto beans and corn kept us going. Enough feed was raised to feed chickens pigs and milk cows. No one suffered for food, at least at our house. This was during the depression years of the thirties; very little money was to be had.

Since our homestead was out of the Cedarvale school district, Oliver Sr. bid in the school bus route, making it legal for us to ride to school. After the two older children finished grade school and talk about Cedarvale loosing its accreditation with the state, the homestead was leased out and the family moved to Encino, until the two older children finished high school.

The homestead was sold and a small ranch at Corona was purchased, making it possible for Sibyl and Shelton to finish high school with students they had started with at Cedarvale, as by this time the school was closed there. The family ranch at Corona was sold when Oliver Sr. died in 1949. Jettie died in 1974 at which time she was living in T. or C., New Mexico.

The Hamilton families, along with many other neighbors remained dear friends through all these years. We have many happy memories of the "Homestead Days."

Clint Smith Family

By Flossie Smith Groffy

Clint B. Smith and his wife, Rosa, with their five children, Willie, Zola, Lester, Gladys and Flossie moved from Graham County, Missouri, to Cedarvale in February of 1910.

They homesteaded on a farm on which there were no improvements. They lived with Ed Smith, C. B.'s brother, until a house could be built. A well was dug which had plenty of water. In fact, Clint furnished water for a good many for his neighbors who didn't have wells.

Clint was a blacksmith and did work for some of the neighbors. They raised corn, but mostly pinto beans. They had their own cream, milk, butter and vegetables. They would take a covered wagon and go to Capitan for apples. They shared harvesting time with their neighbors.

Many times Mrs. Smith delivered babies as the doctor was so far away. Some of the babies would arrive before the doctor did.

The children all went to school in a one-room school house except Flossie, who finished in a new four-room schoolhouse in Cedarvale.

The oldest son, Willie, married a neighbor girl, Nora Tonkinson and settled on their own farm. Zola married a neighbor by the name of Glen Taylor. They also lived on a farm until they moved to Colorado.

Gladys married Barney Welch. They farmed for other people until they moved to Texas. Lester married Lucille Vance and did some farming but moved to towns where he worked.

During a time of seven bad, dry years, Mr. Smith, wife and daughter, Flossie moved to Vaughn, New Mexico, where Mrs. Smith cooked in a hotel. Mr. smith had a blacksmith shop and Flossie worked in a café until she married Fred, (Jack) Groffy and moved to Colorado. She still lives in Pueblo, Colorado, and is the only surviving one of the family.

Four years of work in Vaughn, was followed by the Smiths moving back to Cedarvale and lived until Mrs. Smith's death in 1939. Mr. Smith sold his farm and moved to Colorado to live with his daughter, Zola, until his death in 1943.

Mr. and Mrs. Smith, son Lester and wife Lucille, and Willie and wife Nora all rest in the little cemetery at Cedarvale.

The Harry Smith Family

By Virginia Smith Joplin

Harry Smith homesteaded southwest of Cedarvale in 1909. His family had come to Roswell from Kansas in 1899. Edward L. Smith, Harry's father, helped to lay out the townsite of Cedarvale in 1908 along with L. W. DeWolf and Mr. Taylor.

Pearl, Harry's wife, had a sister in Estancia by the name of Bess Constance, who was ill. In 1912 Pearl came from Iowa to care for her sister. At this time she became acquainted with Harry Smith. She returned to Iowa following the death of her sister but returned to Estancia in 1916 and married Harry.

Harry worked for a time as a conductor on the New Mexico Central Railroad which passed through Cedarvale.

Three children were born to the Smiths: D.H., Virginia and a son who was deceased at eighteen months.

D. H. left in 1939 and Virginia in 1938. Virginia married a man by the name of Joplin. She now lives in Tucson, Arizona, and D. H lives in Farmington. D. H. was a shift supervisor during the construction of Glen Canyon Dam in Arizona.

Nora Smith

In the year of 1895 a baby daughter weighing about four pounds was born to Matthew and Carrie Tonkinson near the town of Springfield, Ohio.

She grew into a teenager and attended school there until she became a young lady at sixteen, then with her parents, two brothers and one sister they left Ohio and came by train to New Mexico and they all homesteaded on claim about four miles southwest of Cedarvale. She was the youngest of four children.

Later on, about a year later a young man from St. Joseph, Missouri, moved to New Mexico and they became sweethearts and were united in marriage on November 28, 1917. After becoming Mrs. W. C. "Bill" Smith they lived on Bill's homestead about eight miles west of Cedarvale. Now known as Leonard Hobbs home place, two children were born while they lived there: Pauline and Frank. They later moved to her father's place with her father, after the death of her mother, then they had two more children, Madiline and Leon.

They lived the rest of their married life there and were very active in the community.

She has been a member of our club here since before she was married and the other activities, they celebrated their fiftieth anniversary while living there in 1967. Bill passed away in 1970. And she continued to live there until her eyesight became so bad she couldn't see "the snakes" then she moved to Weed, N. Mexico, where she now resides, most of the time with her younger son Leon and his wife Merle.

Tonkinson, M. P. Family

By Alice Hileman Ward

Mr. Matthew Peter and Mrs. Carrie Louise McCartney Tonkinson came to Cedarvale by covered wagon from Ohio in 1909. They traveled slowly because of their daughter Nora and son Frank's health, as they had serious cases of asthma.

They homesteaded southwest of Cedarvale about two miles. Nora stayed with her parents but Frank was older so he moved to Raton, New Mexico, and later to Boulder, Colorado. He made his home in Boulder but did not marry until the age of fifty-five. He died in Boulder and is buried there.

The Tonkinsons had four children. Harry Weith was born May 16, 1885, and died September 21, 1968. His wife, Cleah, was born August 8, 1892, and died in 1978. Harry and

Cleah had four children.

One child was born in Cedarvale. She was Anna Marie Tonkinson Ruef. Her birthdate was 1910. Three others were born in Ohio before they left there. They were Elizabeth, Naomi, and Charles.

Frank Tonkinsons and his wife had no children. Edith Bell Tonkinson was born February 29, 1892, and died September 21, 1980. She married Bob Hileman and to them were born nine children.

The M. P. "Pete" Tonkinson's daughter, Nora, was born August 4, 1894, in Ohio and she was almost sixteen years old when she came to Cedarvale in 1909. She lived the remainder of her life in New Mexico most of it at the land near Cedarvale.

Nora had married Bill Smith in 1917. Their children were Pauline, Frank, Madeline and Leon. Leon died in 1986.

Pete Tonkinson and his son, Frank, were blacksmiths, mending wagon wheels, horseshoeing, and everything they could do for other farmers and people around them.

Edith Tonkinson Hileman has twin boys buried in Cedarvale Cemetery. When she first came to Cedarvale she taught school. Vera Foster Barnes was one of her pupils.

William C. Smith Family

By Pauline Smith McCloud

William (Bill) Smith's family moved to Cedarvale in 1910 from Graham County, Missouri. His father was C. B. Smith (Clint) and his mother was Rosa. Bill had three sisters, Zola, Gladys and Flossie, and one brother, Lester.

Bill finished the eighth grade in the little schoolhouse in the timber southwest of Cedarvale, on what is now the Howe Ranch. Nora Tonkinson had come to Cedarvale in 1910 as a girl of sixteen. She and her brother, Frank, had both suffered from asthma in Ohio so they moved to New Mexico. She and Bill were married on November 28, 1917.

Bill and Nora lived on Bill' s homestead, now known as the Leonard Hobbs ranch, on the same location as the present home. They lived there until about 1925 when they moved to the Tonkinson homestead. There were now two children, Pauline and Frank. Pauline was born in 1918 and Frank in 1922. This location was much nearer to school for them. Later two more children were born. Madeline Smith Shannon was born in 1930 and Leon in 1935.

Until Bill's death they remained at the above location. After his death Nora continued to live there until her eyesight failed too much. Then she sold her land and moved to Weed, New Mexico to live with her son, Leon.

Leon passed away in 1986 and then she moved to Cedarvale to live with Pauline until her death on March 25, 1988.

Steiner, William Family

I Lucille (Pyburn) Steiner, was born to Rennie C. Pyburn and Alcy (Brown) Pyburn, on November 29, 1921, having one older sister and two older brothers, on a farm southwest of Estancia.

I attended school at Ewing, Willard and Estancia. We were living two miles west of Estancia, when tragedy struck early in life, Papa passed away in January 1938.

In 1939 I went to Albuquerque to a beauty college, and meet William O. Steiner who was born in Raton, N. M., moved to Albuquerque in his childhood days. He was employed at the Santa Fe Railroad Co. We were married August 31, 1940, at my grandparent's home Mr. and Mrs. E. U. Brown farm south west of Estancia.

To this union two daughters were born. Janet Fay (Steiner) Boyd in 1942, who now lives in Alabama, they have three children. Barbara Kay Steiner born in 1956 attending college in Austin, Texas.

The longest, lonesomest time of my life was when Bill was in the Navy in World War

II, but was fortunate enough to live close enough to mama, and my stepdad Charley E. Clark, they lived on Uncle Johnny's Block farm SW of Estancia and my sister Cecil at Willard, passing the time away until the war was over.

We then went to California, Arizona, Oklahoma, and lived the last ten years in Tahoka and Gragam, Texas. As the "Old saying goes" the chicken's (after forty years) comes home to roost. Bill and I moved back "Home" to Estancia in October 1979 to be near and with my sister Cecil De Vaney, the only survivor of my own family. One stepbrother Walter E. Clark of Albuquerque and one stepsister Alice Mae Whalen of Oregon.

Then in January of 1980 I became a member of the Cedarvale Quilting Club and can truthfully say I look forward to every other Wednesday to visit, quilt, eat, and "chit-chat" with all.

May GOD continue to bless all of us in health and happiness and friendship. "Love you all" it's great to be home in New Mexico.

The Cad Stiggens Family

By Lois Stiggens

Lois Toombs Stiggens was born September 10, 1907, in Belcherville, Texas to the home of George and Kitty Toombs. The George Toombs family moved to Cedarvale in December of 1930. Their furniture was shipped to Torrance by freight car on the New Mexico Central Railway which ran through Cedarvale. The Toombs and Stiggens lived for awhile in the Cedarvale Hotel. For a short time Cad and Lois rented and farmed the P. L. Mitchell place, later moving back to Cedarvale.

For a time Cad drove a school bus. Teachers, Claudia Jensen, Effie Harris and Lena Sanders boarded with the Stiggens. Some years later Lois was postmistress while Cad trucked.

A son, Jerry, was born while the couple were living in New Mexico. Cad and Lois moved to Delta, Colorado, in 1950. Cad passed away there on January 24, 1978, and was buried there. Lois still lives in Delta.

The father of George Toombs, William Linsey Toombs, was born in Mississippi. He was a barber on the Mississippi Queen when he was young. He also moved to Cedarvale and lived on a farm west of there. A son, Bob, lived with him until his death. Bob, later married Miss Addia Dennis, a schoolteacher in the Cedarvale schools.

The Ramon Tenorio Family

By Mary Ann Tenorio

Mary Ann Lucero, daughter of Refugio Lucero married Ramon Tenorio. Both families trace their heritage back some generations in this area. They still live in Cedarvale in what was at one time the home of R. H. Harper, who owned and operated a general store here.

The Luceros were sheep ranchers and their land lay near Corona, Cedarvale and Pino Wells. Mary Ann's grandparents on her mother's side, the Abeytas, were also sheep ranchers.

May Ann has one brother, Pete Lucero and two sisters, Juanita Candelaria and Corine Gallegos.

Ramon also came from a sheep ranching family and the ranch they owned now belongs to Mr. Surratt, located in the Gallina Mountains.

Ramon and Mary Ann are the parents of two daughters, Rachel and Virginia Tenorio Hoak, and three sons, Roman Jr., Richard and Robert.

Mary Ann was a schoolteacher for several years. She and Ramon celebrated forty-nine years of marriage in 1989.

Also, in 1989 the Tenorios were honored at Old Timer's Day in Estancia to represent the county.

I, Mary Ann Lucero Tenorio was born July 4th, 1916, about five miles southeast of Cedarvale. My parents were Refugio Lucero and Antonia Abeyta Lucero. My father was a sheep and cattle rancher we helped with ranch work.

Our land was located near Pino, Cedarvale and Corona. The Lucero ranches are now owned by Wilma J. Davis, Bill Smith, and Bud Bagley. The rock house where I was born still stands and can be seen from the highway on the way to Corona.

My father died in 1933. His death, the depression and the droughts all at the same time brought many loses and many changes but my mother managed to keep us in school and I became a teacher.

In 1940 Roman and I were married. The Luceros and the Tenorios were lifetime friends so I have known Roman all my life. All the Tenorio boys were cowboys which they did for a living.

In 1942 Roman was drafted during World War II. He served three years in the air force in Europe. I had to learn to fix flats, haul wood and water.

Roman and I have five children: Rachel a graduate of C. H. S. and State University in Las Cruces; Virginia a graduate of C. H. S. and business school in Albuquerque; Roman Jr., a graduate of C. H. S. and Western University in Silver City; Richard a graduate of C. H. S. and University of N. M. in Albuquerque; Roberta graduate of C. H. S. and Police Academy in Santa Fe; and one grandson attending school in Albuquerque.

The children are all employed and Roman and I are retired. We enjoy our family, friends and neighbors. And we have enjoyed many trips in the states and in Europe we have reservations to fly to Mexico September 2, 1980, and this is the story of my life.

Toombs, W. L. "Dub"

W. L. Toombs, "Dub", was born in Belcherville, Texas, March 2, 1902, and passed away December 14, 1980. Elsie Cathey Toombs, his wife, was born September 25, 1904, and passed away October 11, 1986.

Three daughters were born to this couple in Ryan, Oklahoma. Dorothy was born February 4, 1924; Billie was born March 11, 1926; and Bobby, on November 25, 1929.

They moved from Fleetwood, Oklahoma, to Cedarvale on Christmas Eve of 1930. They moved into the hotel with Poppa Toombs, George, until a house could be built on the ranch land east of town. "Dub" Elsie and girls lived in a small house on George and Kitty's ranch until Dub homesteaded on land east of Pino Wells.

In 1924 the family made an extended emergency trip to Oklahoma which cost them the homestead. On their return to New Mexico they moved to Estancia and stayed there approximately three years. Then they bought a farm near Pinos Wells and moved again.

A son, Ray, was born there on August 25, 1939. Dorothy and Billie both married in 1942 and left the home. Dub and Elsie moved to Portales where Eddie was born on September 10, 1946.

They again moved back to Cedarvale for a short time and then moved to Santa Fe where they lived their remaining years.

Dorothy married Beryl Gustin August 4, 1942. He was in the service for three years. They now live in Artesia, New Mexico.

Billie married Tommy Keelin on December 24, 1945, and lived in Calton, California. Bobbie married Andy Perez August 4, 1948. Her husband is now deceased and Bobbie lives in Santa Fe.

The Twyeffort Family

By Muriel Twyeffort Pounds

In 1910, Walter Kleinert Twyeffort and Edith Belinda Jones, were married in Valentine, Texas, Big Bend Country, he, a Yankee from Brooklyn New York, came west in about 1904, to become a cowboy. Edith was born in Texas, her young life spent on a back land farm on the river in Lampasas, Texas. Then at age five or six, she resided on her uncle John Means's ranch with five boy cousins and three girl cousins. Her mother had been left a widow at the age of twenty-seven with five children, the youngest being three months old. She ran a boarding house in Valentine for railroad workers. The boarding house was at a division point on the railroad.

In 1914, on the advice of an aunt already homesteading southwest of Estancia, Torrance County, New Mexico, my father, mother and I came to Torrance County. The summer of 1914, papa worked in Algers Sawmill, west of Chilile in the Manzano Mountains. It was lovely. We lived in a slab shack by a tumbling creek with wild strawberries and violets along its banks.

We acquired a black and tan terrier pup and Snow Flake, a lovely milk goat. We always had to have milk for cereal. Mama and I would sometimes walk to the sawmill to watch all the operations. My most vivid memory was watching Mr. Holliday's ox teams hauling the big pine logs down the mountains with the luscious smell of the fresh sawdust. The Olgers who owned the mill, had a big two-story log house. Every now and then they would have a party. Even though I was only three, I had fun.

In September of that same year we boarded the New Mexico Central Railroad in Estancia with various boxes and suitcases the spotted terrier, and the milk goat in the baggage end of one passenger car. We debarked in Cedarvale. The depot was a vacant boxcar. There was no ticket agent, you just paid in cash when you got on the train there.

Cedarvale's only place to spend the night was Mrs. Hileman's about a block south of the depot. She had a long room that was divided off with strung sheets, probably on baling wire, between however many double beds the room would hold. She probably fed us too, but I can't remember eating because I was so interested in sleeping arrangements.

Papa was a friendly, affable person and he rustled around and got acquainted. He located a job teaching the community one-room school, eight grades, about eight miles southwest of Cedarvale. He also located a house for us to live in. It was made of boards, one by twelves, with large cracks between. Was it cold!

The schoolhouse was about three miles south of the Tonkinson place. We lived about three quarters of a mile east of Tonkinson's. Shank' mare was our only mode of transportation, and papa had a healthy walk to and from school, but we had the best neighbors in the whole world, Mr. and Mrs. Tonkinson treated us like family.

Mrs. Tonkinson's biscuits browned more on the bottom, so I'd sit next to Mr. Tonkinson and swap the top of my biscuits for the bottom of his. He couldn't chew too well, so we both profited.

One year they raised a doggie calf on mostly dishwater. Folks made do with whatever was at hand. When you made your own soap you weren't too free with it, so the calf didn't have enough lye soap to keep it from thriving.

On weekends, before papa had enough $30.00-a-month paychecks to buy a horse, he'd borrow a team and wagon and haul us some wood and a barrel of water. Water was scarce and very hard. It wouldn't cook beans, everyone's main food, so we'd catch rainwater and melt snow to cook our beans in.

Papa had good qualifications to teach school, and had he asked he would have been given a lifetime teacher's certificate. However, he'd come out west to be a cowboy. The two teachers who preceded him had been run off by the pupils. So he was somewhat apprehensive but he did real well with them.

When spring came and school was out, Papa filed on 320 acres south of the Pino Mountains, six miles north of Cedarvale. He bought a one-room, well-built shack from Dr. Ewing's homestead, south of Cedarvale for $30.00 (to be paid in $3.00 monthly installments) Dr. Ewing was Torrance County's dentist for many years. With the neighbors' good help, Papa moved the house to the south of the Pino Mountain. We had no well or fence.

In order to comply with the homestead laws, you or a family member had to live on the land for three years, plow and plant two acres the first year, and plant another twenty more the following year. New Mexico land has a very loose and thin topsoil in most locations. When cultivated, the top soil soon blows away with the heavy spring winds, which I've seen blow steady for three months in the spring. The plowed land soon loses all its ability to produce crops.

Some places, such as draws and land close to the mountains had better soil, but ours was very poor. As my father had never farmed, he never raised any crops to amount to much.

Papa put a two wire fence around the little field, and I had fun running behind his walking plow when he broke sod, gathering the fat white grubs in a can to feed to the turkey and a few baby chicks. The damp, cool earth felt so good on pink, bare feet; the only time I ever enjoyed being barefooted.

The first winter south of Cedarvale had fun memories. On Sunday we had Sunday school in the little schoolhouse. We'd walk, but someone would generally give us a lift part way home, oftentimes the Fosters. They were so kind, as were all the neighbors.

Glen Taylor was courting Zola Smith. He had a high stepping black horse and a swell black buggy with a black top. Real sporty it was, Mr. Foster had a wagon and a fast team always ready to run. After Sunday school they raced down a lane lined with stumps to dodge. We'd be in the Foster's wagon hanging on and bouncing while Mrs. Foster would be hollering for Ottis to stop. He'd be grinning and urging the team on. Glenn's girl would be hanging on trying to grin but looking pretty scared. It was fun anyway.

We had a Halloween party (pie party) in the old schoolhouse once. My proper mother dressed up in black like a witch and read palms. I remember the frightened or pleased looks in the teenagers as they came out of her corner. Mama didn't make a pie for me, she made a custard, and a little boy I couldn't stand ate it with me. Or, at least I guess he did. I had my back turned while eating and when I turned around the pie was gone.

Mama and I lived alone from Sunday afternoons to Friday afternoons. At that time we would drive the fifteen miles to pick papa up. He would haul wood, and a barrel or two of water for us.

Mama was never afraid of man or beast, subsequently, that trait had been handed on down. So passed the homestead years.

One of those summers Papa went back to Brooklyn, N.Y., to see his mother. He had a short, fat sister, Nellie Twyeffort, that came to keep Mama company while he was gone. Papa bought an eight-or ten-foot square tent and built a floor and four walls to stretch the tent over. This made a room for aunt Nellie.

It was fun to have company, especially an old maid aunt with beaux that sent boxes of candy on a regular basis. Every time we traveled Aunt Nellie wore high heels. Then we'd have to walk home. She also had a lovely red wool sweater, and every time she wore it, it would rain and the sweater would fade on her.

Before she left she gave papa $25.00 to buy lumber to build a shed kitchen on our one room. And when she got back to Brooklyn, I guess she told Grandma Twyeffort about the sad, wobbly wheels on the buggy, because she bought us a two-horse buckboard.

Between school terms Papa taught a short term west of us about three miles at the Ramon Tenorio ranch so passed the three years necessary to live out time on a homestead.

We got our patent signed by Woodrow Wilson for the place. Our homestead had no well, so Papa sold it to P. L. Mitchell, a neighbor to the south, for $1,600.00, then Papa bought the Markham homestead a mile west of us. It had a large room with three "shed rooms" adjoining the back, a well of water, and a two wire fence enclosing the 320 acres. It was mostly sandy timber of pinon and cedar.

In the meantime a baby boy, Ben, joined our family. Papa went to work in Willard for the Hanlon Mercantile Company for the winter of 1918–19. It was a most severe winter as the snows were frequent and deep. Restrictions were on food stuffs and coal and heating oil the terrible flu epidemic raged on.

My mother had been raised a Baptist and my father a Presbyterian. In the fall of 1918 a traveling evangelist of the church of the Nazarene came to Willard and held an evangelistic campaign in which my parents were converted to and joined in, the church of the Nazarene.

The following spring some evangelists came to Cedarvale and held a revival campaign in a brush arbor on the Cad Livingston place. Enough people were converted to organize a church. It was at this time my father felt it God's will to be a minister. He studied and was soon an ordained minister. He was never a regular pastor; he filled in here and there on Sundays as a sort of circuit rider. He performed lots of marriages and buried many people. He taught school in the winter and tried to make a crop of beans in the summer (not very successful). Anyhow, we had lots of string beans and roasting ears to eat. It was mighty good eating.

I attended my first school in Willard at the age of eight years. A Mrs. Vigil was my teacher and she taught me phonics thoroughly. She made reading and spelling so easy for me.

I rode a school bus through the fifth, sixth and seventh grades. The buses were some Dodge trucks with a body built under a wooden top, heavy mesh wire sides, wooden sitting benches along the side, a heavy oil cloth to let down during the cold weather, and a chain across the back to keep the kids from falling out. We carried our lunches to school in Mary Jane Syrup pails or lard buckets.

In 1918 or 1919 Cedarvale's new schoolhouse was built. It was made of hollow red tile made at the N. M. penitentiary. It consisted of four big rooms, a hall lined with lockers, and folding doors between two of the rooms which, when closed, made a nice auditorium.

We had no playground equipment so we played Black Man, Flying Dutchman, Pop the Whip, spun tops, and played jacks and hopscotch.

The teachers never seemed to have any discipline problems. School was too valuable to not appreciate it. Our best entertainment in the classroom was a spelldown or arithmetic match on Friday afternoons after recess. Competition was real keen.

Outside the school we had two three holers—one male, one female (restrooms.) outside, a big cistern caught rain water, (drained through charcoal) for the five gallon water coolers in the hall. The big boys filled them every day. Big pot bellied cast iron heaters kept us warm.

When sickness came, the neighbors helped in any way possible. Mrs. Fletcher and Mrs. Foster knew lots of remedies and were generous with their knowledge and time.

When death arrived, a coffin came from the general store, either in Willard or Corona. They cost $40.00 for the regular size. The neighbor men dug the grave which was very hard digging since the graveyard site sits in caliche rock. Sometimes the rock had to be dynamited everyone contributed food to the house of mourning. Mrs. Foster generally "laid out" the corpse, meaning washing and dressing, etc., then two more neighbors "sat up" with the corpse. Grief was shared.

Weddings were generally trips to Estancia (the county seat) for a marriage license, then to the judge for the exchanging of vows. As soon as the news flew around the "charivari" was organized. Neighbors gathered after the couple supposedly feel asleep and made all the racket possible, ringing bells, beating tubs, etc. until the groom came out and invited them in to his house and his pocketbook.

Lots of homesteaders were able to weather the lean years by milking cows and selling the cream. The Laval cream separators were used to separate the cream from the fresh milk. They were hard to turn and a mess to wash up as they had abut forty or fifty parts. The skim milk went to feed the calves, a few hogs, chickens and kids. The cream was collected in five-gallon tin milk cans and shipped to Denver, Colorado. The cream checks financed groceries, taxes, and other things. I've seen women tote a five gallon cream can, full, on horseback, six miles to be shipped.

Bean harvest was a stressful time before proper harvesting machinery came along. When ripe, the row of beans were plowed up. What ones were missed were pulled by hand and all were put in piles about ten feet apart. Talk about a backbreaking job! Folks who want to exercise and lose their tummy fat ought to try pulling beans. As soon as the piles were dry, they were pitchfork tossed into a wagon with racks on the sides, hauled to the corral and stacked to await the threshing crews. Five cents a pound was a good price for beans.

Everyone made most of their clothes, bedclothes, soap and bread. People raised their own chickens, butchered their own livestock and were pretty self-sufficient.

We went to church when we could. Our entertainment was going to Cedarvale once a week for the mail, maybe some matches or soda and slap some baking powder. It was a gentle way of life.

In the last part of 1927 I met a newcomer to the community, Tom Pounds, son of E. E. Pounds of Coldwater, Kansas. He purchased the old Victor Lenares ranch headquarters. It was located five and a half miles west and a little south of Cedarvale. I was sixteen years old, but in those days there weren't enough women to go around, so few were allowed to become old maids.

After a most determined courtship, we were married. On October 16, 1927, my father conducted the ceremony at home. After dinner we went over the hill to the Lenare's place he fixed a flat and I entertained an old lady who came to call, a Mrs. Lucero. She was surprised to find no people celebrating. Her husband herded sheep for us and kindly helped me. Sometimes.

Those were most interesting years. We

were very green, in experience and in trusting. There are just no words to describe us, but we learned.

After the crash of 1929, Tom's father went broke so we bought the headquarters place; paid four-fifths of it and took seven years to pay off the remaining one fifth. We had fifty cows, twenty-five heifers, and 680 sheep to start with. The first year about half of the cows died with blood poisoning after calving. One year we had $600.00 total income. We learned one lesson well, don't spend more than you have in your hand.

We always had plenty to eat in the hard years, though it wasn't what we would rather eat. We had a big eighteen-quart pressure cooker and would can meat in the fall. I baked our bread and also bread for the sheep camp. This usually amounted to eight big loaves every day.

We couldn't afford a camp cook. Part of the time we couldn't afford a herder, so we had to herd all the sheep. After four years or so we sold the sheep and bought a little more land and a $40.00 gasoline washing machine. Part of the time in the 1930s we had no money to buy gas for the Model A we had, so we went with the wagon or an old spring buckboard and Jake and Kate, the mules. We sold eggs for three cents a dozen, yearlings for six cents a pound, and when calves made it to ten cents a pound we felt pretty lucky.

In 1934 it didn't rain until the 26th of August. The cows lived on soap weed that winter. We weaned what calves we had on soap weeds and hauled them to the corral. Some of them died, but those which survived surely made rustling cows.

It has been a mighty interesting life, and anyway it was never dull.

My three children, Maxine Brown and her husband Jim, Steve Pounds and his wife Myla, and Thomasine Romans and her husband, Milton and two girls live only a few miles from the ranch home.

The Vickrey Family

By Pamela A. Vickrey and Nolan J.

Adam Northrop Vickrey was born in Tennessee and came to Torrance County from Waxahache, Texas. He filed on the homestead five miles southwest of Cedarvale on December 20, 1911. He established his residence on this land February 16, 1912, with his wife, Mary Elizabeth Kendricks Vickrey and his youngest son, Charlie E. Vickrey. A grandchild, Eloise Woods, who was the child of a deceased daughter, Alice Carolina Vickrey Woods, also lived with them.

The eldest son of Adam and Mary, John Cleveland Vickrey, homesteaded on the adjoining property in 1912. John resided there until the 1920s with his wife Ena Swafford Vickrey and six children: Lorene, Minnie, Joe, Violet, Viola, Alfre, and John. This family moved to Whitharrel, Texas, where John resided until his death. His homestead is still owned by his children who live in Texas.

Charlie Edgar Vickrey, the youngest son, married Maggie E. Meyers. Their children were three sons, Everett Goliad, born in 1920, Nolan J. born in 1922, and Allen Norwood born in 1932. The homesteads of Adam N. Vickrey and some adjoining land are owned by Nolan J. who lives on the land, and his daughter, Pamela A. who is a teacher in Farmington, New Mexico.

The Meyers family of William A. Meyers and his wife, Mildren Norwood Meyers moved to Torrance County to homestead from Nolan county, Texas, near Dallas in 1911. William homesteaded land four and one-half miles south of Cedarvale near the Cougar Mountain. May Meyers Moseley, Ed Meyers, Ethel Meyers Stroope, Maggie Earl Meyers Vickrey and Mildred Meyers Lee were their children in chronological order.

May and Boyd Moseley lived in the Cedarvale vicinity until the early 1950s when they moved to El Paso, Texas. They had three children: Charlie, who is deceased, and Bill and Dorothy Kiely who live in El Paso. Their last home in the community still stands in Cedarvale across the highway from Pauline McCloud's house.

Ethel Meyers Stroop married Ab Stroop and lived in the area. They had one daughter, Zelpha. They all died while living in Corona.

Ab's early property was south of Cougar Mountain, now known as the Stroop well. Ethel's homestead was north of Cougar Mountain. Later they moved to the old Walton place by the double wells near Cedarvale.

Maggie E. Meyers Vickrey homesteaded six miles southwest of Cedarvale. She married Charlie E. Vickrey in 1919. The members of their family are listed with those of Adam Northrop Vickrey. Everett and his family live in Alamorgordo area and Allen Norwood and his family live in Taos, New Mexico.

Nolan Vickrey

Born of Cedarvale on June 14, 1922, with Charles and Maggie Vickrey. Married first wife Lola February 15, 1944, had one daughter, Pamela, not married! She died of Leukemia in May 1987.

Grandparents; Myers. Stay area and ranch mom and dad's homestead, jack of all trades and master of none.

Remarried December 30, '88, Zelma. She has two children, Tommy and Pamela.

Clint Welch

By Ruth Campbell (Welch)

Clint Welch was born October 19, 1885 in Commanche County, Texas. He married Emma Letz who was born December 2, 1896, in Bastrop county, Texas. They were married on August 15, 1915.

They moved to Cedarvale, New Mexico, in the winter of 1915–1916 where they homesteaded with Clint's parents west of Cedarvale. They lived there a few years and then moved east to a farm which they rented from Willie (Bill) Smith. It is here where most of the children were born, bringing the total to ten.

Nett Clint, January 3, 1917. Married Juanita Minor, three children.

Sumpter Carl, August 24, 1919. Deceased November 13, 1933.

Nelson Eldridge, May 23, 1920. Married Lydia Kenyon, three children: Nelson, deceased November 12, 1961, Lydia deceased September 19, 1968

Emma Ruth, May 19, 1922. Married David Campbell, three children

Ida Mae, September 26, 1924. Married Eugene Dawsonl seven children: one child deceased June 19, 1972, Eugene deceased June 23, 1975.

Asa Harold, July 8, 1926. Married Sadie Yancey, three children: Asa deceased January 22, 1967.

Calvin Lee , May 21, 1928. Married Pauline Wood, three children.

Matthew Peterson, December 27, 1930. Married Willie Dee McCloud, three children.

Minnie Alice, August 5, 1932. Married Kenneth Alberson, five children: Kenneth deceased March 28, 1967, Minnie married Lewis Topliff.

Lonnie Wayne, August 28, 1935. Married Nellie Blake, two children.

In 1937 they purchased land west of Pinos Wells where they continued to live, calling this home. Clint had driven a school bus to Cedarvale prior to moving and continued driving from this place for many years to Duran, Cedarvale, and Corona. The family raised sheep, farmed and milked cows, selling the cream.

Clint died April 4, 1957. Emma continued to live on the farm approximately one year at which time she sold to the Abeyta family and moved to Alamorgordo where she lived until she passed away on May 5, 1987.

Emma was honored at her funeral with all of her living children present. A grandson, the Reverend Donald Welch, gave the eulogy. Some of her grandchildren sang and some of the grandsons carried her casket.

All of the Welch descendants consider it an honor to have had such devoted, hardworking and exemplary parents.

Edna I. Wright

I, Edna Irene Wright, was born in Dawson County, Texas, January 18, 1911. My parents, Mr. and Mrs. William M. Wright, nine brothers, two sisters, and myself came to New Mexico by covered wagon, driving our stock, the fall of 1916.

We rented the Medcalf place, where we farmed until Dad filed on land and we had our own home. My dad and mother belonged to the Primitive Baptist Church and my dad preached part time. I went to school at Progresso and Cedervale.

Charlie Gonce came from Mineral Wells, Texas, in 1930 to share crop with Fat Elliston. We met and were later married on February 1, 1932. To our union was born a daughter Charlotte Mae and six years later a son, William Leonard. Our daughter married Nathan Strong, they had two sons. Nathan passed away in 1969. Our son married Judy (Hodgin) and they have two children, a daughter and son.

We share cropped with Mr. Jockey for two years, then rented the Beedle place for about three years. We then worked for Mrs. Osborne for about one and a half years. In 1938 and '39 we rented the Jockey place again. In 1940 and '41 we rented the Bob Elliston place, while there we bought land and built our home on it, where we are still living. Our family all are members of the Southern Baptist Church. We have four grand children and three great grandchildren.

Wright's Reunion

The family of Francies and William M. Wright gathered at the home of Mr. and Mrs. Charlie Gonce of Willard May 8th and 9th for a family reunion. It was the first time since 1923 for such a gathering and those who attended reminisced and visited about past family history. The family first came to Willard area in 1916 from Dawson County Texas, near La Mana. They traveled in three covered wagons, with the older boys driving the livestock. The youngsters all attended the one-room log cabin schoolhouse, in Progresso.

As they came of age the older boys and one sister Willie Mae homesteaded land, in the area. Of the original twelve children the seven survivors meeting here are: A. Ray Wright, Geo. V. Wright both from Bisbee, Arizona. Frances (Susie) Cole from Shelton, Washington, Loman C. Wright from Hilmar, Calif., Willie Mae Shay, Marvin Wright both of Belen, N. M. Edna I Gonce of Willard, New Mexico.

Other family members attending were: Mrs. Vernon Wright of Denver, Colo., Mrs. Ray Wright, Mrs. Geo. Wright, Charlie Gonce, Mr. and Mrs. Don Coker, Rickey, Mickey and Marshal Piztman, Scot Coker, Mr. and Mrs. Al. L. Wright, Lias Writh, Bruce Wrightr, Mrs. Henery Cram, Mr. and Mrs. Frank Wright, Kevin Wright, Karen Wright, Mr. and Mrs. Dec Willbank, Mike Willbank, of Rheme, Texas.

Friends visiting the family during the reunion were: Mr. and Mrs. Leonard Hobbs, Mr. and Mrs. Ray DeVaney, Mr. and Mrs. Elmer Devaney, Mr. and Mrs. Paul Lackey, Mrs. Ethel Lackey, Mr. and Mrs. James Hansen, Alice Hansen, Mr. and Mrs. Roy Humphries and Marsha Humphries.

History of the Cedarvale Quilting Club

The sewing club, now known as the Cedarvale Quilting Club, is the oldest club in Torrance County. It was organized in 1916.

The club consisted of a group of church ladies who quilted for each other. They met in the homes of the members and served potluck dinners. At first they met every two weeks. The quilting bee was a time to meet, have fun and also accomplish some worthwhile task.

The club also helped the community and the school with their projects.

In 1940 they held their meetings in the old Baptist Church building. Later they traded this building to Ramon Tenorio for a house where they met for many years.

In 1953 when the Cedarvale School consolidated with the Corona School, the club met in the kitchen and dining room of the schoolhouse. The building began to deteriorate, making it too cold and uncomfortable for the ladies to meet in it. In 1980, the old Pythian Sisters building was purchased and renovated. The ladies held may dinners, box suppers and quilted many quilts for pay in order to complete the renovation. The quiltings are now held there weekly. Some of the first members were Carrie Tonkinson, Nora Smith, Maggie Vickery, Ethel Stroope, Mae Mosley, Mildred Gee, Evalena Belzer, Effie Foster, and Pallie Dishman. All of these ladies have passed away, but their daughters and granddaughters are still quilting and enjoying the tradition they handed down.

It has been estimated that over 2,000 quilts have been quilted by the Quilting Club. Over the past few years many women have belonged to the club.

Obtained by me from my Aunt Martha Piggott Hobbs from the quilting show held in Corona in 1988

How To Make a Friendship Quilt

"A Friendship Quilt"

Back in the late 1920s when Progresso was a thriving community, the ladies, for a pastime, would make a friendship block and exchange with neighbors. The blocks of this quilt were a prized collection of one of the earlier settlers, Mrs. Guy Osborne. Being unable to complete the quilt, she gave the blocks to her very good friend, Edna Gonce. Edna saved her flour sacks, bleached them, and used them for the lining.

Edna set it together and quilted it herself. It is one of Edna's most treasured quilts.

—Submitted by Edna Grace

"A Friendship Quilt"

The submissions about friendship quilts were taken from a booklet at a 1988 quilt show given by the Cedarvale Quilters in Corona.

Cedarvale Quilters in front of schoolhouse circa 1970

Quilt shown on previous page designed and quilted by Cedarvale Quilting Club, entitled "Blocks of New Mexico"

We give special thanks to Grace Lackey for making the nametags for us. Grace has been a member of our club for many years, but because of ill health she no longer can meet with us even though she is confined to a wheel chair, her mind and hands are always busy.

THANKS GRACE

Old friends get together at schoolhouse for quilting. L–R: Iva Humphries Hobbs, Jeannette Piggott Webb, Edna Wright Gonce, Grace Humphries Lackey, with curious kids from California in the background.

Quilts Displayed at 1988 Quilt Show

(1)The History of "Star Daisy"

My mother, Willie Ann Griffin, designed and started this quilt in 1906 as a young bride. She used an eight point star diamond to shape into a flower petal and a collection of small scraps from two or three generations found in her mothers and grandmothers quilt scrap boxes. She was followed by four generations to furnish scraps later.

It is a string quilt pattern in the quilt world and holds many memories of the past—good and bad times—but lots of love, friendship, joy and happiness.

The first twelve blocks and a few scraps of previous years were carefully kept for many, many years. I found them on a trip to my old home at Hunt, Texas, and mother was glad to have me take them to finish. It was such a pleasure to get it finally finished then quilted by the Cedarvale Quilting Club in 1977.

I, Edna Robinson, am dedicating the quilt in love to the memory of Willie Ann Griffin, 1886–1987, and ever gratefully praise Cedarvale Quilting Club for their lovely quilting.

—Edna Robinson

(2) "Blessed are the Quilters for they are Piece Makers"

Senior Class of 1937: Estancia, N. M.

My dad smoked R. J. R. tobacco which came in white sacks. I cleaned the sacks, cut the white strips, and took them to school. I asked each class member to write their own name and position they held as a class officer. It took the faculty and janitor to complete the quilt top.

I embroidered all names and helped mother piece the top and mother quilted it for me.

This quilt is not a piece of art, but is a *great treasure* to me.

—Cecil B. (Pyburn) DeVaney

(3) " Six Point Star"

The Six Point Star belongs to Hazel Burton, Corona, New Mexico.

It was pieced by my grandmother, Callie Taylor from Clovis, New Mexico. She gave me the top about twenty-five years ago. Not knowing how to quilt, I put it away in my cedar chest until I moved to this area and I joined the Cedarvale group of quilters about five years ago. It was a joy to see it finally made into a quilt.

—Hazel Burton

(4) "Flower Basket"

This quilt belongs to Willa Mae Bonham of Santa Fe, New Mexico. We do not know the age, but it belonged to Fannie Wilson, who passed away this year at the age of seventy-eight, and she made it many years ago.

(5) "Tulip Basket"

This quilt belongs to Willa Mae Bonham of Santa Fe, New Mexico. It was a gift from her friend Fannie Wilson. We do not know anything about this quilt except it is quite old.

—Willa Mae Bonham

(6) "Penguin Quilt"

This quilt was made by Bonnie Thomas for her daughter Tammie. The Cedarvale Quilters did the quilting.

Tammie's favorite colors are red and black and she collects penguins. She has always wanted to go to California to see the palm trees, so we quilted palm trees highlighted by the glowing sun.

—Bonnie Thomas

(7) "Dutch Doll Quilt"

This quilt was made by each person who

has their name on the block and quilted by the same and given to Nora Smith. She in turn gave it to Pauline McCloud to be hers after she was gone.

—Submitted by Pauline McCloud

(8) "Lone Star Quilt"

The Star was pieced by Annie McCloud out of her quilt scraps, put together by Pauline McCloud. The pieced Star was given to Gayle McCloud as a birthday gift.

—Submitted by Pauline McCloud

(9) "The Twist Quilt"

This quilt was pieced and quilted by Evelyn Campbell and was just a pattern she liked.

—Evelyn Campbell

(10) "Annie's Flower Garden Quilt"

This quilt was pieced and quilted by Evelyn Campbell. It was just a pattern she wanted to do.

—Evelyn Campbell

(11) " Rose Quilt"

This quilt was made and quilted by Mrs. L. O. (Effie) Foster and when she was in her late '80s.

—Submitted by Helen Livingston

(12) "Rainbow Quilt"

This was made by Mrs. L. O. (Effie) Foster and was quilted by Helen (Foster) Livingston and Mrs. L. O. Foster in 1938.

—Submitted by Helen Livingston

(13) "A Friendship Quilt"

For many years Iva Hobbs collected friendship quilt blocks. It was the fad many years ago to give a special friend a block you made with your name on it. When she had collected enough to make a quilt, she set them together and also quilted it herself. Most of the ladies that made the blocks have passed away. Iva has passed away, but the quilt has a special place in the home of her family.

—Submitted by Martha Hobbs

(14) " Rose Flower Garden"

The Rose Flower Garden with the fence was a treasure of Iva Hobbs.

(15) "Donkey Quilt"

The donkey Quilt was pieced and quilted by Iva Hobbs in about 1957. There are forty-five square print blocks which make up the donkey.

The donkey consists of 4 solid color square blocks, 25 triangle blocks of coordinating colors, and 1 white triangle. These are put together in a larger block with enough square blocks and triangle blocks to make a 20 by 24 inch block. It takes twelve blocks to make a quilt 83 by 90 inches. The many rows of quilting makes it look very complicated.

—Submitted by Martha Hobbs

(16) "Cowboy Quilt"

The Little Cowboy Quilt was made by Jane Lamb. It is appliquéd and then tacked. Makes a very good quilt for a little boy to cuddle in.

Also makes a nice wall hanging in a young man's room.

—Submitted by Martha Hobbs

(17) "Lone Star"

This quilt was pieced and quilted by Della Piggott. Della pieced and quilted many quilts. This is the last one she did a month before she had a stroke which paralyzed her right side.

This was a special anniversary gift to her daughter, Martha Hobbs.

(18) "Greek Cross Sampler"

Michele Rose designed and pieced this quilt. Jimmie Wells drew the quilting design and quilted it.

—Submitted by Michele Rose

(20) "Lone Star Quilt"

This quilt was pieced in the 1890s by Frances Dobbs Collins and Mary Frances Collins Mathiese, who were great grandmother and grandmother of Mary Jo Hopson.

—Submitted by Mary Jo Hopson

(21) "Moorish Motif"

This was pieced by Zelfa Atkinson. Pallie Dishman did a lot of the quilting. This pattern is known by other names such as Love Ring. The same pieces can be put together in a different design and is called Drunkard's Path.

—Submitted by Zelfa Atkinson

(22) " Giant Dahlia Quilt"

This was pieced by Sarah Elizabeth Dishman in 1934. Mrs. Dishman was in her late eightys at the time she made this quilt. She never allowed anyone else to cut a piece for any of her quilts and always pieced them by hand. It was quilted by the Cedarvale Club and bound by hand by Pallie Dishman. It is owned by Day Lindsey, great granddaughter of the creator of the quilt and granddaughter of Pallie Dishman who was a member of the Cedarvale quilting group for about sixty years.

—Submitted by Kay Lindsey

(23) "Friendship Quilt"

Back in the late 1920s when Progresso was a thriving community, the ladies, for a pastime, would make a friendship block and exchange with neighbors. The blocks of this quilt were a prized collection of one of the earlier settlers, Mrs. Guy Osborne. Being unable to complete the quilt, she gave the blocks to her very good friend Edna Gonce. Edna saved her flour sacks, bleached them, and used them for the lining.

Edna set it together and quilted it herself. It is one of Edna's most treasured quilts.

—Submitted by Edna Gonce

Progresso

Progresso was a stop on the New Mexico Central Railroad which ran between Santa Fe in the north and Torrance where it made connection with the Southern Pacific-Rock Island Lines. A boxcar station and water tank stood beside the tracks and there was one train each way daily. Most of the trading was done in Willard which was a junction point of the New Mexico Central and Santa Fe railroads. A country store and post office in Progresso were run by Mr. Boone. Aside from the store , Progresso was composed only of a Roman Catholic Chapel, a one-room schoolhouse and three or four ranch houses at the foot of the Rattlesnake hills.

The few families in the community were faced with the problem of school for their children occasioned in part by the widely scattered population (no busing then). Toward spring, four families in the rural area south of Progresso formed a subscription school, for three months, with one of the mothers, Mrs. Guy Beedle, as teacher. Classes were held in a dugout. The following summer men of the community hauled logs from the Gallinas Mountain and built a schoolhouse on a "school section" which was set aside by the government for support of the public schools when established. The floor was dirt and the room was heated

Progresso July picnic 1917. An original at the Palace of the Governors, Santa Fe.

by a wood-burning stove. Each family constructed desks for their children. Again it was a subscription school with Mrs. Beedle as teacher. About a dozen families were involved in the payment of the teacher for a term of six months. A year later a new district was opened in Progresso, and all children attended the one-room school. This term was for eight months.

Colonel J. Francisco Chavez was the owner of a large sheep ranch at Progresso at the time of the founding of Torrance County. The first county seat was at Progresso, where the only buildings were those of Col. Chavez' Ranch. On January 1, 1905, the Santa Fe Railroad sent a special train to Progresso with a passenger car to serve as a "Courthouse-on-wheels." It was several years later that Colonel was murdered.

Information furnished by Alfred W Hurst and taken from a paper by Gladys Corbett Orme. Reproduced from History of Torrance County, New Mexico.

At the post office, Progresso, N.M., c. 1917. (Courtesy Gail D'Arcy)

At the Progresso Store, c.1917.. (Courtesy Gail D'Arcy)

Progresso picnic, c. 1917.

Staley's Homestead. Front: L–R Jeannette Piggott, Louise Gustin, Martha Piggott. Back: Verne Piggott, Della Piggott holding Bertie Lee Piggott.

Playing house at Louise Gustin's

Windmill post card, Message on back reads: "This was taken at Mr. Staley's Place—see the Mesa."

B. E. Piggott Family

Following are Conversations Bertie Lee Piggott Johnson had with her sisters, Jeannette, Martha, and Viola (nickname: Polly).

About Mom (Della Piggott)

"Della's mother was Sarah Jane Hutchins Ogden. She sewed on a treadle machine. She sewed for other people to help with income especially after her first husband, Mahlon Vestal Hutchins was killed in 1907 (he was killed along with two other fellows when a railroad handcar they were operating collided with a train). Sometimes when she was very tired one of the children would sit on the floor and pump the foot pedal." Della, Mattie Dell Hutchins, was born in North Carolina. The family located in the area between Lane and Beagle, Kansas. They were Quakers and attended the little Friend's Church in Lane.

Della's Wedding Dress

She married at age sixteen. Her dress was a silver grey (taffeta, I think). It had small vertical tucks in the bodice. It was made by her mother, Sarah Jane, who become a seamstress as she was a single parent much of her adult life. She and Edgar Piggott went to Paola, Kansas to get married—brother Willard and wife Mable went with them. They went by train to Colorado Springs for their honeymoon.

Bert Edgar Piggott who was always known as Edgar or B.E. was born and raised in the area around Osawatomie Kansas. He had four brothers, Willard, Otis, Harry and George. Like their father, Herman Sherman Piggott, they were railroad men with the exception of George who lost his eyesight due to accidents.

In 1909 Edgar and Della wed; Edgar made several trips to New Mexico before bringing his wife and two small children to New Mexico in 1913 beginning their homsteaders' life.

Since "Dady," Edgar, had to hold his seniority on the railroad, the family had to return to El Reno, Oklahoma every so many months—yet they had to live on the ranch so many months to "prove up" on the claim.

About 1916, Della and children were alone on the ranch. Ruth (as in Aunt Ruth Hutchins, Della's sister) had come by train to visit. Verne was at school. Della, Ruth and children (Jeannette and Martha) went to visit neighbors—the Frevert family. He (Verne) had been instructed that if no one was home when he got there, "go to the phone and ring his own phone signal (such as two longs and two shorts) and wherever Mama (Della) was she would answer and tell him what to do." This time she told him where she was and he started to go there, but somehow he confused the Frevert place with the Staley place so he went the wrong way. It was getting dark. Della and Ruth started home but did not meet him en route by the time they arrived home, Della put the lamp in the window and she was preparing to hunt for him when he came crawling through the fence, crying. When he got about halfway to the Staley place he realized his mistake and turned back. He was safe at home, after such a scare. Della fainted later at the supper table.

In approximately 1918 or 1919, Edgar had gone to Amarillo, Texas, to work. Della and the children (Verne, Jeannette, and Martha) had passes to join him. Time to go, wood supply was gone, but train could not get through for days because of snow. Neighbors offered for them to stay at their houses—White family—lived about a half mile north in a half-dug out house. Della hesitated because the families' character was a little questionable. But no other choice, so they stayed two or three days until the

The Piggott family, circa 1929.

	Born	*Died*	*Married*
Bert Edgar Piggott	10/13/1888	04/1963	06/12/1909
Mattie Dell Hutchins (Della) Piggott	08/27/1899	10//1971	
Verne Vestal	04/02/1910	02/1984	
Fern Jeannette	03/21/1913	11/2006	
Martha Maywood	07/11/1915	06/2003	
Della Viola	03/08/1920	03/1993	
Bertie Lee Etta	09/18/1922		
James Otis	06/19/1929	07/1983	

train came through Progresso—but it took the train three days to get from Progresso to Torrance.

About 1921, Christmas—not much money—Christmas Eve a big snow. Edgar knew the children knew the situation yet he knew they would be disappointed in the morning if sox were empty. He rode horseback to the Progresso General and got candy and an orange for each child's stocking.

1922, Bertie Lee's birth. Dr Wiggins came from Estancia by buggy; he worked all night trying to deliver the baby. Sometime in the wee hours—the children (Verne, Jeannette, and Martha) were awakened and told to walk across the pasture to the Beedle ranch. They arrived there about sunrise, feet wet with dew. Beedle's fed them breakfast then took them by home (by wagon) to get

Piggott's homesteader ranchhouse near Progresso, circa 1920.

school clothes, by then the baby had arrived. It took so long because the umbilical cord was wrapped around baby's neck twice. Mother and baby survived, could not hear baby cry in the other room for days.

One-room school. One teacher, Mrs. Ward, would throw erasers at students. Two big boys sat in front of room. Verne and Ike Mulkey and two DeVaney boys in back. They picked the adobe (mud) out from between logs and used corset stays to flip at each other. Little ones between had to dodge!

There was a general store at Progresso, it had the post office too. Mr. and Mrs. Pierce were owners. They had a little girl about the same age as Viola and the gossip was the child belonged to a neighbor.

The White family had a daughter named Linnie, a little bit "flirtatious," rumors were she was pregnant; she supposedly took her own life. She is buried about three quarters of a mile east of the old school house location. This was White's property then. Martha says a few years ago some of the White family came to find her grave and to mark it.

Roy Elliston and Rufus Humphries both liked Aunt Ruth (Della Piggott's sister) when she came to visit. They got into a fight one time during a "dance." "Daddy" sent everyone home after the fight."

Roy Elliston was a brother to Rob Elliston who was married to Frazier Bell Elliston. They came to New Mexico right after they were married, he was thirty-two and she was just sixteen. It was a treat to stay all night with them. Frazier B. was so much fun. She would sneak into our room at night and scare us. She never wore shoes and she could pinch with her toes, under the table when we were eating. They had one son, Bobby, who died when he was eight years old with appendicitis. We were living in Wichita and we always got the Estancia paper. I remember Dady reading it and he came into the kitchen to tell mother that Bobby had died. Right away my family went because mother and Frazier Bell were so close. The evening that we got there, Frazier B was out walking and she and mother cried. It seems that Roy Humphries along with someone else, had sent us a telegram from Willard because Frazier B. was sure that mother would come to be with her at the funeral. We never got the telegram. After that, they couldn't stay there; they moved to Albuquerque. I think that Rob sold farms and houses. I think later that Leonard Hobbs owned their ranch.

Rob's brother came there about the same time, the only name we knew for him was "Fat" and his wife was Artie. They had a little boy, the same age as Bobby and I think they had a little girl.

The DeVaneys—his name was Sheridan and we called him Shady. Their children were Jessie, a girl, then Elmer, who married Cecil, Donald, and I think there was another child. I remember when the quilt club finished a quilt at their house they took it outside and Donald had a cat with a leg off in a gunny sack, he dumped him onto the quilt to see who would get married next—the two ladies where the cat ran between them were the fortunate ones.

Later Elmer and Cecil had five children. The store, the general store, in Willard (the Moorfields lived in the house next to their general store), when their son, Fowler Moorefield and his wife, Uthabell, ran the store she told us that when Cecil got thirsty for strawberry pop she knew that Cecil was pregnant.

At school one day, Martha wrote a note to Kenneth Beedle. It fell on the floor, teacher, Mr. Dunlap found it. He gave it to Jeannette to show to Dady. Dady made Martha read it to him and then gave her a spanking.

Old "hermit" named Cagle lived in a dug out, a little southwest of DeVaney homestead, near the mesa. No one knew much about him. No animals of any kind, not even a dog or mule. His dug out burned some time after 1926, no one knew what happened and no one seemed to know about his history.

Man named Uncle Charlie ran a little store by the railroad track.

Jeannette and Martha were riding a horse named "Dick," a black horse, to school. After school, they rode a ways with Marguerite Mulkey. He got restless while the girls talked, kept prancing. When they were ready to go, Jeannette had become provoked with him, she gave him a kick in the ribs. He took off so fast that Martha fell off the back and when she left his back, he stopped so quick Jeannette went off over his head. Jeannette was holding a birdcage, Martha had a lunch pail.

The Mulkeys—they had a son we called Ike and a daughter, Marguerite. After we left New Mexico and were living at 1424 St. Francis in Wichita, Kansas, Marguerite ran away from home. She put her clothes in a bag outside the house when she went to the field. We are not sure if she walked or rode a horse to the train depot in Progresso and came to our house. She got a job and she met Barry Cramer and married him. They had the first radio and we used to visit them on Saturday nights to hear the radio. Jeannette was so popular everywhere she went and I remember that Ike rode his motorcycle all the way from New Mexico and he brought her a ring, her birthstone. At that time, her birthstone was called a bloodstone (which was pretty ugly) but it changed later.

Mr. And Mrs. Jockey were one of the families that were there before 1929. They were from another country. I could never understand them when they were talking.

I remember that the people sometimes had dances on Saturday night in someone's house—someone had a wind-up phonograph—usually there was some food, too.

In 1929, Jim was just six weeks old when mother and the family went to the ranch for the summer. The Humphries family and our family went to the Gallinas on a big hayrack. It took most of the first day to get there, we cooked our supper on a bonfire. After dark we sat around the campfire and told stories about mountain lions, etc. and we all slept together on the hayrack. It was cold and the stars were so bright. In the morning, the two Lackey boys (Paul and Raymond) came riding up on their horses to climb up the mountains with us. Mr. Humphries, mother and Jim and I stayed at the camp. I wanted to go but mother said I was too young—I was seven. Viola went but she got so tired. They went to the top and across the other side and to the sawmill. The Humphries always brought some lemons along because there was a soda water spring near there and they always made lemonade. This is the time that Paul and Grace met and a romance was started (Paul started courting her—he would ride his horse those twenty miles to her house on every other Sunday afternoon). When they got back to camp it was late in the afternoon, mother had some supper ready for us and it was time to go home. It was late at night, and no street-lights to show the way—we had our lanterns on the wagon and we would sing all the way back home. This was always our treat for every summer. Usually we had to pick out a day when it had been raining and the fields were too muddy to work. We just picked up the food that we already had—mother (or Aunt Maggie—later) made pancakes, biscuits, etc.

Their Children:

Verne Vestal Piggott married Gladys. Children: Patty and Jack

Fern *Jeannette* Piggott married Clayton D'Arcy. Children: Gail, Roland, John (Jack)

Divorced, married Clifton G. Webb

Martha Maywood Piggott Miller married Wildy Miller. Children: Lanee', Kay, Jane

Husband died, married Leonard Hobbs of New Mexico (after his wife Iva died)

Della *Viola* Piggott Atkinson married O. Dean Atkinson. Children: Jim, Gary, Sandy

Bertie Lee Etta Piggott Johnson married Calvin Johnson. Children: Kermit, Donna, Lisa, Cindy, Erin

James (*Jim*) Otis Piggott married Gerda. Children: Sharon, Elfriede

Divorced, married Janice

Following are some sketches of what I know from my grandparents, the B.E. Piggott's or think that I remember; as my son David used to say "you can only see things with your own eyes" and these are mine.

The Piggott's remained in Wichita where Edgar worked at the railroad roundhouse as a machinist until such time that Grandpa Piggott, Edgar's dad, was becoming feeble. So, Edgar, Della, son Jim and I moved to Osawatomie to live with Grandpa. (I was about seven years old at the time and was staying with them. Jim was high school age). Edgar worked nights at the railroad roundhouse in Osawatomie. Grandpa died. I returned to California with my parents. Jim graduated OHS where he played football, same as his father. Edgar retires from the railroad.

Meanwhile in New Mexico, the ranch was leased to different people. For quite some time, Della's sister, Maggie, and her husband, Pete Moore managed the farming at the Piggott ranch. One of their daughters married Howard Gustin. When Edgar retired, he and Della decide to return to the New Mexico homestead. This is in the early 1950s. There is electricity but no running water or indoor facilities. Close neighbors included the Hansons, Mary Ellen and James and Mary Ellen's children Charles David and Judy Hodgins, and the Gonces, Edna (Wright) and Charlie and their son Leonard.

These were the main playmates of us Piggott grandchildren. Also, about our ages were the DeVaney children and Paul and Grace Lackey's boys (in fact Lanee', Martha's daughter, married the second oldest son, Archie), and Pansy Hobbs daughter of Iva and Leonard Hobbs. During the summers, we watched (probably thought we were helping) the Lackeys and others brand and inspect their cattle.

In 1957 when, I believe, Grandmother, Della Piggott, was becoming tired of the wind, the dirt, and the isolation, the Piggotts had a farm auction and sold the ranch to Charlie and Edna Gonce. Eventually, their son, Leonard who married their neighbor Judy Hodgins, acquired the old Piggott place. Leonard and Judy had two children. Leonard was a sheriff's deputy who was killed in a vehicular accident. Enter, Leroy Humphries, son of Roy and Grace Humphries who has a doctorate and has done well in Nashville, Tennessee. Leroy, the grandson of the original homesteaders, has the dream and the ability to fulfill his father's yearnings to own all that area including the Piggott ranch which he purchased from Judy Gonce.

As of this writing, 2009, the Piggott's old house is still standing and with Leroy Humphries permission, the Piggott grandchildren still visit. There is just something about the land and the spirit there that binds us.

After Della and Edgar Piggott sold their New Mexico place, they moved to Kentucky to be closer to their daughter, Martha

In 2000, I sat down with my mother: F. Jeannette Piggott D'Arcy Webb

(Note: it seems that many in our family were called by their given middle names)

I was born March 21, 1913, in El Reno, Oklahoma, where my dad was working for the Rock Island railroad.

We left there when I was two weeks old, then, I think that we went to New Mexico taking the train to Progresso.

In New Mexico our transportation consisted of a mule team and a lumber wagon. Brother Verne was run over by wagon at age three and broke his leg, we were hauling water from DeVaney's.

Verne was three years older than me.

First attended school in Estancia, first grade promoted to third grade.

School at the ranch was a one-room log structure, later built one room frame next to it. Original school was at corner of Piggott property (on left of road before the lane). Later moved the frame building over to the south end of "Daddy's" ranch and later used for Sunday school and church.

One year, not enough kids, so teacher and his wife lived in log building.

"My fourth grade teacher, Miss Hill, was my favorite teacher. We had first thru twelfth grades Some boys were nearly grown men! Hard to handle!"

Left New Mexico and went to Salida, Colorado, I attended sixth grade. Dad worked for D&RG Railroad. I took some piano lessons.

Back to New Mexico seventh grade.

Left New Mexico for the last time, went to Wichita, started eighth grade, thirteen years old.

Our family consisted of six children, my brother, Verne, was the oldest. I was the second child; born in 1913, then Martha, Viola, Bertie Lee and Jim. Lost a child between Bertie Lee and Jim born in 1929. The MD came to house, "Mother was hemorrhaging, so the doctor took care of Mother and some say he didn't get the baby started good enough." This child was a twelve pound boy named Sherman Edgar—he is buried in the same cemetery as the folks in Wichita.

F. Jeannette Webb, ninety-three, of

Marysville died November 14, 2006, at The Fountains in Yuba City, California. She was a Yuba-Sutter resident for fifty-six years. She was a member of the First Christian Church in Marysville and several square dance groups. Survivors include her husband Clifton Webb of Marysville, a daughter, Gail D'Arcy of Oroville; two sons, Roland D'Arcy of Browns Valley and John D'Arcy of Maple Ridge, British Columbia, Canada; a stepson, Henry Webb of Tennessee; two stepdaughters, Mary Jo Clark of Florida and Frieda Creagan of Colorado; a sister Bertie Lee Johnson of Kansas; nine grandchildren; seven step-grandchildren; twenty-three great-grandchildren; and a great-great-grandchild.

It seems appropriate that I should fill in some of the blanks between 1913 and 2006 and perhaps add a few personal notes. As of this writing the year is 2009.

In Wichita, mother, Jeannette, went to North Valley High School, after graduation she attended Friend's University and worked at Kresse's 5 and Dime Store. She and brother Verne using railroad passes, compliments of Dady, went to San Francisco to attend a Baptist convention where she met Clayton D'Arcy. And although it seems she had plenty of beaus back home, Clayton pursued her and eventually she took the train to California and they were wed in 1934. Clayton was a railroad machinist, also, and worked for the Western Pacific Railroad. They lived in Keddie (I was born in Portola as that is where the WPRR Hosp was located), moved to Quincy, built a house, where Roland was born in 1940 and Jack in 1942. Then to Richmond; WWII was on. Throughout these years and those that follow, my dear Grandmother Piggott would come by train to California, visit and return to Kansas with me. Around 1946, Jeannette and Clayton divorced. Jeannette and children moved to Marysville and then back to

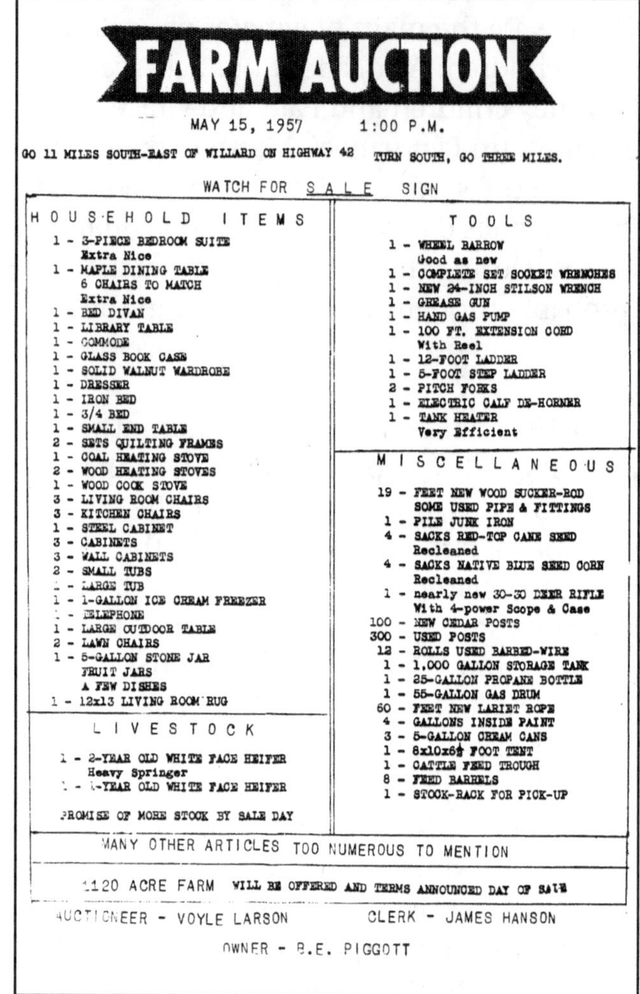

FARM AUCTION

MAY 15, 1957 1:00 P.M.

GO 11 MILES SOUTH-EAST OF WILLARD ON HIGHWAY 42 TURN SOUTH, GO THREE MILES.

WATCH FOR SALE SIGN

HOUSEHOLD ITEMS

1 - 3-PIECE BEDROOM SUITE Extra Nice
1 - MAPLE DINING TABLE 6 CHAIRS TO MATCH Extra Nice
1 - BED DIVAN
1 - LIBRARY TABLE
1 - COMMODE
1 - GLASS BOOK CASE
1 - SOLID WALNUT WARDROBE
1 - DRESSER
1 - IRON BED
1 - 3/4 BED
1 - SMALL END TABLE
2 - SETS QUILTING FRAMES
1 - COAL HEATING STOVE
2 - WOOD HEATING STOVES
1 - WOOD COOK STOVE
3 - LIVING ROOM CHAIRS
3 - KITCHEN CHAIRS
1 - STEEL CABINET
3 - CABINETS
3 - WALL CABINETS
2 - SMALL TUBS
1 - LARGE TUB
1 - 1-GALLON ICE CREAM FREEZER
1 - TELEPHONE
1 - LARGE OUTDOOR TABLE
2 - LAWN CHAIRS
1 - 5-GALLON STONE JAR
FRUIT JARS
A FEW DISHES
1 - 12x13 LIVING ROOM RUG

LIVESTOCK

1 - 2-YEAR OLD WHITE FACE HEIFER Heavy Springer
1 - 1-YEAR OLD WHITE FACE HEIFER

PROMISE OF MORE STOCK BY SALE DAY

TOOLS

1 - WHEEL BARROW Good as new
1 - COMPLETE SET SOCKET WRENCHES
1 - NEW 24-INCH STILSON WRENCH
1 - GREASE GUN
1 - HAND GAS PUMP
1 - 100 FT. EXTENSION CORD With Reel
1 - 12-FOOT LADDER
1 - 5-FOOT STEP LADDER
2 - PITCH FORKS
1 - ELECTRIC CALF DE-HORNER
1 - TANK HEATER Very Efficient

MISCELLANEOUS

19 - FEET NEW WOOD SUCKER-ROD
SOME USED PIPE & FITTINGS
1 - PILE JUNK IRON
4 - SACKS RED-TOP CANE SEED Recleaned
4 - SACKS NATIVE BLUE SEED CORN Recleaned
1 - nearly new 30-30 DEER RIFLE With 4-power Scope & Case
100 - NEW CEDAR POSTS
300 - USED POSTS
12 - ROLLS USED BARBED-WIRE
1 - 1,000 GALLON STORAGE TANK
1 - 25-GALLON PROPANE BOTTLE
1 - 55-GALLON GAS DRUM
60 - FEET NEW LARIET ROPE
4 - GALLONS INSIDE PAINT
3 - 5-GALLON CREAM CANS
1 - 8x10x6½ FOOT TENT
1 - CATTLE FEED TROUGH
8 - FEED BARRELS
1 - STOCK-RACK FOR PICK-UP

MANY OTHER ARTICLES TOO NUMEROUS TO MENTION

1120 ACRE FARM WILL BE OFFERED AND TERMS ANNOUNCED DAY OF SALE

AUCTIONEER - VOYLE LARSON CLERK - JAMES HANSON

OWNER - B.E. PIGGOTT

Photocopy of Piggott's farm auction flyer.

Osawatomie, Kansas, to live with the Della and Edgar, our grandparents. Two and one-half years later we returned to live in Marysville and remained there from that time on. Jeannette married Clifton Webb.

In 1934, after Jeannette and Clayton were married, her sisters often visited. This resulted in several moving to California. Martha married Wildy Miller who was from Kentucky. Clayton secured him a job working for the WPRR, so they moved to Quincy where they raised their family before returning to Kentucky. Viola, the next sister in line, met and married a Keddie railroad man, O. Dean Atkinson who was first a fireman and then an engineer. Viola and Bertie Lee were teenagers at this time and recall

Della and Edgar Piggott in Wichita, Kansas, with Lanee' Miller and Gail D'Arcy, granddaughters.

This is Doris and Gail at the ranch with Grandpa in back.

Granddad Piggott in pick-up, 1954. (photos courtesy Gail D'Arcy)

Some Piggotts and Lackeys circa 1952 including, Edgar and Della, Martha and Wlldy, and three daughters, Gail and Kermit; Grace and Paul Lackey with six sons

Neighbors gathered at the Piggott's for baptism in the old water tank, August 1954.

Della and Edgar Piggott at their back door, August 1955.

late night musical gatherings with some of the local talent around Keddie and Quincy. Bertie Lee, however, returned to Kansas and married Calvin Johnson.

After Martha Piggott Miller's husband died, she returned to New Mexico, buying a home in Moriarity. Leonard Hobb's wife Iva (formerly Humphries) died. Leonard and Martha married, she went to his place near Cedarvale to live. Martha became very active in the community, acquiring the building in Cedarvale for the Senior Center. In fact, so worthy were her efforts that one year the Governor awarded her the "Outstanding Volunteer of New Mexico." Eventually, Leonard became ill and was placed in a facility. Martha returned to Kentucky and died there.

With the exception of the youngest girl, Bertie Lee Johnson, the remaining Piggott children have passed away. Verne who attended Friend's U. in Wichita, became a pilot who instructed Army Air Corp recruits just as we were getting into WWII. Viola, a beautician by trade, is best remembered for her kind spirit and Christian ways; she was very active in the Christian Women's Club. Jim, the youngest, attended college and then served twenty years in the Navy before going back to NMU in Albuquerque where he was majoring in and enjoying archeology when he developed and succumbed to cancer.

Humphries, Piggotts, Wrights, 1929.

Humphries and Piggotts going to the Gallinas Mountains, 1929.

On the hay wagon at the Gallinas, Mountains. Front: L–R: Roy Humphries, Jeannette Piggott, Bertie Lee and Viola Piggott, Ivy or Grace Humphries, Della Piggott with baby Jim, Mr. John Humphries and Mr. Lackey. Back: Martha Piggott and Alma Humphries, 1929.

Jeannette Piggott and Roy Humphries on a mule with a hat.

Grace, Martha, Alma, Jeannette, Edna Wright, Iva.

Mock holdup alongside the puddle jumper rail car. Mrs. Moorfield and Verne Piggott.

At the Mesa after Sunday dinner with the Wrights, circa 1929.

Iva Humphries Hobbs

By Iva Humphries Hobbs

Cedarvale, New Mexico
July 5, 1966

My dear great nephew John, about one and one half years ago, your daddy asked me to jot down all I could remember about your Great Grand Father (after whom you were named) on your daddy's side of the family. Well his full name was the same as yours, John Wesley Humphries. He was born in Kentucky on October 22, 1871, and his father's name was Sam Humphries, his mother's name was Melinda Humphries, I can't recall their middles names. Although, I'm sure I've heard them.

Well your great grandfather was the oldest child of a family of ten children. Here are their names John Wesley = Luttia Alma = Tennessee (called Tennie) = Kansas = Virginia (called Jennie). Then came four more boys Charlie = Irvin, Ruffus and Jeff.

Your great grandfather's daddy was a Baptist preacher and a good one they claimed. He also kept a country grocery store, at what they called Plumbers Landing.

Your great grandfather was a handsome child with beautiful blue eyes and golden curly hair and your great-great grandmother's pride and joy. So she refused to let GG Grandfather cut it. So one day when GG Grandmother was away from home, GG Grandfather got the job done. I don't know, but I imagine there were a great many tears shed that day. G Grandfather was __ years old when they cut his hair. Your GG Grandmother lived in a house back of the store. In those days people didn't have refrigerators or deep freezers. So they put up fish and cucumber pickles and the like for sale in half-bushel wooden buckets packed in salt water (we call it brine) really and did Great Grandfather love to eat those fish when they were cooked. The buckets of fish and pickles and barrels of sugar and barrels of flour stood on the floor of the warehouse in the back of the store. So every time G Grandpa could, he slipped to the warehouse, pulled a big fish from the brine, and would take it home, dragging it in the dirt as he went, because he was such a little boy still, and his little dress would be soaked with brine.

As he grew older and his sisters came to take their place in the family, then great grand father got to go visit his grandparents and he said he used to sleep late while there and when he woke up, his grandmother would give him a cold biscuit with cold coffee and sugar over them for his breakfast. One day when he woke up, he heard Grandma say there is no cold coffee for John's breakfast. Some neighbors were there, they said, just pour a little warm water over the coffee grounds, he'll never know the difference. So she did. A long time afterward she again said there is not any cold coffee for your breakfast. So he surprised her by saying, "Oh just pour a little warm water over the grounds, I'll never know the difference." He said that when Grandma got a meal ready, the last thing she did was to take the coffee pot off the wood stove, and set it on a mat on the table by her plate. Like Mother, in my day, set a large pitcher of sweet milk or butter milk by her plate, then she could refill the children's glasses without having to jump up every time one of a large family of children wanted some. So great Grandfather would watch his grandma and when she got the coffee pot, he'd say "Grandpa, dinner is ready the coffee pot has come."

He said, as he grew older he hated for Saturday to come because he had to take all the white oak chairs out on the back porch and scour them. He said they had to be clean too before he could quit.

As he grew older, he had to stay at home and help his father in the store and help do chores and everywhere he was needed.

Sometimes his father would take him on trips, traveling on horseback to buy cattle. He would buy poor cattle cheap and take them home, fatten them and butcher them and sell the meat. He said lots of times he'd watch close where they went, because sometimes your Great Great Grandpa would say, "John, you take these cattle back home, and I'll go on and try to buy some more. It was in Kentucky near and around Morehead, Kentucky. There were lots of mountains and hills and trees. Not many fences, the trails or wagon roads were dim. In those days folks didn't brand or earmark their cattle like folks do in the western cow country nowadays. So he had to know his cattle by looks and color. He had a bill of sale describing them. So he had to know the cattle by the way they looked and their color. Many times he had to pass herds of other cattle and he must not leave his or take anyone else's cattle

Your great grandpa and his sisters were always busy. Busy people are happy people. They had to get up early in the morning and set out tobacco plants (tobacco was their money crop) in the spring of the year.

Later, they had to pick tobacco worms off the plants and chop out the weeds with a hoe. They also had to hoe the weeds out of the corn. One day Great Grandpa had company. It was a cloudy damp day and Great Grandpa and his sisters had to snap corn. So as they worked they decided to play a trick on Great Great Grandpa. They knew he had a fire in the heat stove in the front room. So Great Grandpa climbed on top of the house and his sisters handed him some gunnysacks. He carefully stuffed them in the top of the stovepipe. He quickly climbed down and away they all ran back to the cornfield. Soon the stove began to smoke (of course) and Great Great Grandpa and his company couldn't stay in the house. Of course, G.G. Grandpa soon discovered what had happened. Great Grandpa didn't say they got a whipping but he made them very sorry for the way they had acted.

Great Grandpa said well, I did some things when I was young that most boys don't get to do. I went to my grandpa and grandma infare dinner, I don't know whether it was the grandpa or grandma that had passed away and the other remarried again. (Infare means wedding reception). Then sadness came into their home, their baby sister, Jenny died with whopping cough. Not long after four younger boys began to come into the home. The five sisters were next to your grandpa, and then came Charlie, Irvin, Ruffus and Jeff. When Jeff wasn't but six or seven years old Great Great Grandfather died. I never knew what caused his death. Now, your great grandpa being a young man, had to take full responsibility of the large family. He had heard of open land in the west. So he brought his mother four brothers and four remaining sisters and came to Netawaka, Kansas. Not enough money to go further. So he stopped and rented a corn farm. He had brought their household goods, furniture, harness, teams and wagons and plow tools with them. He began to raise bumper corn crops and good gardens; bought a few cows and hogs and was getting along good for a young man. Then sister Kansas died. I don't know from what. Great Grandfather had left behind him in Kentucky his boyhood sweetheart, a Miss Nora Ellen Wright. He thought of her often but had the large family to take care of. So he just waited and the years passed by. Then, Tennie and Virginia died, not at the same time. Then sister Luttia married and moved into a home with her husband Dave Lyons and her two stepsons Clyde and Delbert.

Now Great Grandpa had bought into the hog business. He raised his hogs and feed, and sold many dollars worth of hogs. He longed for a home of his own, now being near thirty years of age. Still, he had the responsibilities of his mother and four brothers. He spent a good deal of his time trying to figure out what he could do to support his mother and brothers and yet have his own home, the boys were thirteen, fifteen, and nineteen. So he decided to buy a hotel in Netawaka, Kansas. So he did and moved his mother and brothers there. So she could run the hotel and the boys could help her and go to school.

He had been corresponding with the old sweetheart who had not married but was still waiting for him. So, he made a trip back and paid her a visit. Things were still solid with them and after a short renewed courtship, they were married. If I remember right in September 1904. They took their honeymoon by train, they went to St. Louis, Missouri, to the World's Fair. Then to the Kansas cornfield to start their own life. They were very busy and very happy.

They worked very hard and found that Great Great Grandmother still needed help. So sister Luttia, a blessing to them, flew in and helped your great grandmother. They did all the fruit and vegetable canning for the hotel and furnished garden stuff, chickens and cured meat as well as beef. Besides caring for their own families. The boys didn't like town. So as soon as school was out, they'd come to the farm. This made so much more work for your great grandmother, washing, ironing, and cooking. But the brothers were good help in the cornfield. Then in August 1, 1905, your great aunt Alma was born. Two years later your great aunt Iva Florence (yours truly) was born on December 1, 1907. Two years later your grandpa Roy Marshall Humphries was born, October 21, 1909. Along about this time your great-great uncle Charlie married a girl named Maud, and your great grandmother Nora Ellen took tuberculosis. She was very sick in bed. So your great grandpa got the doctor. They said you "you must move her as soon as you can arrange it to a high climate, New Mexico or Texas."

So Great Grandpa came to New Mexico and filed on a claim that was in 1909, late. Then in August 1910 after the corn crop was laid by, Great Grandfather loaded a boxcar with one milk cow (named Pide), her calf, a pair of mules, one dog, Fido, the chickens, his harness saddle and farm tools. In another car all the household goods, canned stuff, bedding, and came with us all to New Mexico. New Mexico was still just a territory. We spent the first night at a hotel in Torrance, New Mexico. Then we came to Progresso, New Mexico. We landed here August 10, 1910; your grandpa was about nine months old.

All the neighbors were at Progresso to meet us. They had their wagons and teams to haul things to the claim. The neighbors were Shady DeVaney, Fred Frevert, Guy Beedle, and several others. Then, there were more Spanish speaking people than white people. The Spanish people stood back and looked at us through spyglasses. The claim or homestead was about three miles from Progresso. The neighbors helped put up the big tent and moved everything in. They put up the bed and put Great Grandmother to bed to rest. Then Great Grandpa hired a woman by the name of Murphy to take care of Great Grandma and the three children, and he hired a man named Earn Blevens to help cut cedar post and they fenced the half section first to keep the cow and mules at home. First they only put up one barbwire. The woman named Murphy didn't keep us kids clean or comb our hair. Great Grandpa said that woman couldn't even cook beans.

They weren't used to high winds, one day a wind came and blew the tent pole down and it barely missed Grandpa's Roy's head. It fell across the table and broke nearly all of Great Grandmother's dishes. They had bunches of cherries on them. Some day when you are at your Great Aunt Grace Lackey's house, she will show you a tiny butter plate. It's all that is left of the set. Great Grandpa had left his hotel for the great-great grandmother to use, but he still owned it. It's still standing at this time, June 9, 1967. He also left men who promised to harvest his corn crop. Corn in that part of Kansas is snapped in August. It was too late to put in a crop here.

So as soon as the fence was up. Great Grandpa bought lumber, rough lumber meaning "not planed" and built a two-roomed house. That's one of the first things I can remember, is the New House. I would be three yrs old in December of 1910. I was so glad of the house. I can remember the holes for windows with no glass yet and no doors. Then they put in the windows and doors and covered the outside with tar paper (black tar paper). Then, they moved us in. Then he used the scrap lumber and built an outdoor toilet and a barn and a chicken house of pinion poles.

There was no well yet. So we hauled water three or four wooden barrels from a

Spanish neighbor—named Spedian Lewaris. We hauled in a wagon with the mules to pull the wagon. There were lots of wild animals, as the country was just being settled, coyotes would howl at night. But we were not afraid. One morning our parents had us look out of the window and we saw three coyotes. They had a poor little jackrabbit cornered between them and they caught it. There were a lot of bobcats (still are) and porcupines. One night after Great Grandmother was well (she got well fast), she got better each day, she was cooking bacon for supper and a bobcat got on top of the house. I can still hear it cry. It smelled the meat, I guess.

One night Great Grandfather was coming home on horseback. He had bought two white mares, for an extra team to work. Their names were Fanny and Nellie and a panther follow him all the way home. It was dark. It screamed and just sounded like a woman screaming. Us kids were really afraid that night.

Then Great Grandpa began to break up the soil getting ready to plant a crop the following spring.

One day the next spring Great Aunt Alma and Great Aunt Iva went for a walk with Great Grand Mother's umbrella. A whirlwind came and turned it wrong side out and ruined it. It was a black one. We had many neighbors, a family on every half section. Here are some of their names (we could see the lights at night from some of their windows, we all used coal oil lamps). Mr. Kirchoff, Mr. Shady DeVaney, Mr. Guy Beedle, Mr. Geiger, Mr. Jack Hurst, Mr. Metcalf, Mr. Boone, (he kept the store and post office at Progresso; he was the only one married to a Spanish wife) Mr. White, Mr. Fred Frevert, Mr. Kelcy, Mr. Blevens, Mr. Myres, Mr. Pucket, Mr. Mulkey, Mr. Staley, Mr. Downes, Mr. Sheen, Mr. Hyhole, Mr. Piggott, Mr. Ward, many more but these were the closest, Mr. Jockey, Mr. Nieme', the last two are Fin people.

We began to raise good crops. We raised pinto beans for a money crop millet, corn and cane for grain crops for feed. We all stayed well until 1913 when your great aunt Melinda Gladys was born May 10, 1915. There wasn't a doctor, so they had a midwife and something went wrong. She got infection in the naval cord; died on May 21, 1913. How sad we all were. They buried her about a quarter of a mile north of the house in a snow white ruffled casket that the neighbors made. That is where the present Humphries Cemetery still is. But just before this your great-great uncle Irvin took T.B. and G.G. Grandmother brought him to New Mexico thinking he'd get well like G.G. Grandmother Nora Ellen did, and while here G.G. Grandmother proved up on half section of land north of G.G.pa's land. Later your G. Grandpa bought that half section. G.G. Uncle Irvin became worse and G.G. grandmother took him home to Kansas to die and be buried.

In 1914 Great Grandpa and the neighbors drilled a well on the north east corner of the section (the homestead). They used horse for power to drill the well. He had drilled two wells previously to this time, but failed to find water. This time he succeeded so he moved our house and all our things to the well. Then Happy Day, they, G.G. pa and the neighbors put up the windmill on the wooden tower. I remember that day for I was six and a half years old by then. A house belonging to a Spanish family just one and three quarters of a mile north of us burned down. We were all out watching the men put up the tower and the windmill and when they finished they climbed up and turned the wheel by hand to see if it would pump. Great Aunt Alma saw the water begin to come and she ran fast to the house, grabbed the water bucket, threw out all the water and came to catch water from the well. She did but it was muddy and had oil in it. So we couldn't drink it. The neighbors and their families went home and as tired as Great Grandpa was he caught up the horses, harnessed them, hooked them to the wagon and we all went with him and hauled our last load of water. We hauled it from Spedion Lurens. We had white neighbors on the south and west of us and Spanish neighbors on the east and north of us. All of them good neighbors. The Spanish sheepherders loved us kids and every summer they'd give each of us an orphan lamb or goat. So Great Grandpa decided he'd take our pet goats named (mine) Katie Did, (Alma's) Nancy and (Roy's) Joe, to the sawmill at the Gallinas Mountains and trade them for lumber to build two more rooms on our house.

While he was gone a Spanish lady went crazy and wandered from home and we could see north of us people, we couldn't see the people just the light of the lanterns all over the hills searching for her. Mamma and us kids were afraid. So we blew out the coal-oil lamps and watched from the windows, we went to bed early. They found her about 1 o'clock in the morning. At that time the Santa Fe Railroad ran about one and a half miles north of us. It is now Highway 42. We always loved to see the train go by and hear the whistle blow. By this time we had several mares and young colts. When the whistle blew the colts would come running home.

After we built the new rooms and before we began to use them, in the spring G Grandmother put setting hens and their chickens out there. One day Grandfather Roy stepped on one and out ran all the yellow. He grabbed it up and said, "don't worry mamma, I'll put it back."

The Spanish people herded sheep all around us. The young boy herders would come to the house for fresh water and cookies. They gave us a lot of orphan lambs and goats. So we'd raise them and have mutton to eat.

Then in the spring of 1915, Great Grandpa was breaking a colt to ride. He rode her one morning to Progresso to pay the Pole tax. An hour or so later, the colt came home hard as she could run. Down at Progresso, there was, and still is, a house in which Fredrick Valesques lived. Their dogs run out and scared the colt. She threw G Grandpa and in pawing at the dogs, she pawed G Grandpa in the head, neck, and back. Mrs. Valesques saw and run out with a broom and drove the pony away or she might have killed him. She run to the store about a half mile and got help. They brought G Grandpa home in a wagon. G Grandma had run that way to see about him. She told us kids not to come with her. Tell John that the mare was safe at home, she said. Mama met him halfway, about. They told her he is OK but he had both his legs and both his arms broken.

But when they got home they walked him into the house and held him by his arms. Mamma sent them after the white neighbors. He was unconscious for about thirty-six. The folks had a bunch of cows and were milking and selling cream to town. So the neighbors took turns milking and taking the cream to town. In about three weeks G Grandpa was able to help haul hay. During the time G. Grandpa was sick, Grandpa Roy was five then or would be in October. So he saw a herd of sheep. He told the neighbor boy Hugh White go bring them home. I don't see a herder and they said for us to have all the sheep without a herder, because the coyotes would eat them.

Then good times came again, good rain, lots of grass, fat cattle, good crops and on October 25, 1916, your great aunt Grace Lackey was born. Then in 1918, we had a drought. We didn't raise a crop and so could put up no feed for the cattle in the winter. It was a terrible winter so so cold and so much snow. We lost most of our cattle because we had grain ordered but trains could not come through. Some got too weak to get up and froze to death. We skinned them and in the spring we sold $93.00 worth of hides.

Every one, everywhere had the bad flu that winter. Many whole families died with it. Your G. Grandmother, Great Aunt Alma, Grandpa Roy, also, Great Aunt Grace had it. But Great Grandpa and Great Aunt Iva didn't take it. Finally the snow melted and the trains came through and we got to the station at Progresso and got the corn we'd ordered and didn't loose another cow. We cut wood with a crosscut saw. Butchered the fat young calves for meat, had plenty beans and canned garden stuff to eat. We had a happy time to know all our family lived through the bad flu. The reason the calves were fat, because they sucked the cows, the meat would freeze solid on the north side of the house and would keep fine. We chopped soap weeds, Yuca you call it, and split the roots and it made good cow feed. The cattle that lived had such sore feet; they would leave trails of blood on the snow and ice.

But now we were faced by World War I and your Great Great Uncle Ruffes was one that went. Now food became scarce and flour and sugar were rationed. We had to eat cornbread most all the time and I don't like cornbread much to this very day. Then the war ended and rain came, things and prices became normal. We raised good crops again. Us kids were old enough to help in the fields and garden. Great Grandpa bought more land, as several of the neighbors went broke and left the country. Great Grandpa and other neighbors bought their land, so they'd have money to go somewhere else.

All this time us kids kept going to school in the little log schoolhouse with one teacher, thirty-two children in all. So we continued with our education. (I have a picture of the little log schoolhouse, I'll loan to you to have one made for your book, if you like). The log schoolhouse was built by all the fathers in the center of the community. We had our first school in it in about 1914, I think. Before that, we kids and some other neighbor children walked to a neighbors house a Mrs. Guy Beedle, she taught three of her own children also. Great Grandpa paid her $1.00 a month for each of us. Her three: Esther Emma Beedle, Osborne Beedle and Margaret Nell Beedle. Also, she taught Albert Mulkey and Margueritte Mulkey. The people all had Sunday school and church in first one home and then another, until the log school house was built. At first, we only had a dirt floor, we finally got an organ. The first song I remember was "When the Roll is Called Up Yonder." So the years passed. Hard work, but happy days mostly. The neighbor children had fun spending Sundays and some times nights together.

Then on November 5, 1926, sadness again came into our home. Great Grandmother took sick with a cold, which ran into pneumonia, and after about three weeks, she passed away.

We didn't want to go to school. We always missed the first part of the school year up until the harvest was over and we had to work like beavers to catch up and pass the examinations on the first half of the books. But Great Grandpa said you kids must finish your education like your mother and I planned. It seemed like the end of the world had come when she died. The dry years and drought had caused many families to have to leave. So we no longer had enough children for a school. So our school was closed in about 1924. We didn't go to school at all in 1924, so that made all of us a year older than the others in our class. Your Great Aunt Grace was barely ten years old when Mamma died so it was hardest of all on her.

Anyway, Great Grandpa went to Willard and rented a little white house and moved us and a wood cook stove, beds, a table and our clothes up to Willard to go to school there. We were so lonely since Mama had only been gone one week. We hated the loneliness and even the town. But the people and teachers were kind and finally we began to live again. Great Grandpa was more lonely than us being all alone. So he hired a man and woman to come and work for him all winter and spring, a Mr. And Mrs. Dude Wright. There was a high school there so we went to school there the rest of 1926, 1927, 1928, 1929, 1930, 1931. Four years until Alma, Iva and Roy graduated from high school and Great Aunt Grace graduated from the eighth grade. Great Grandpa received an honor award and we were all real proud of him. Then we got a school bus route established and Great Aunt Grace went to Willard all through her four hears of high school on a school bus, sixteen miles, morning and night. During all the summers we'd work at home in the fields and garden and house, helping raise the crops and harvest them. We bought more land and Great Grandpa got it all paid for.

During this time your Grandpa Roy was going to college at the University of Albuquerque. One year the second, he didn't have enough money and had to stay home one year and work. Then in the spring of the year 1936, your Grandpa Roy graduated from the U of N.M.

To think back it was a lot of fun and happy days going to school in the little log schoolhouse in the center of the community. All the kids walked to school. We had to walk two miles straight west. One or two years we had an old bay horse named Dan. We'd hitch him to the buggy. One day your Great Grandma Nora Ellen Humphries gave your Grandpa Roy and I, six dozen eggs and told us to hitch up old Dan and go to the store and post office. We were to buy each of us, Alma, Iva, Roy, and Grace, a new little brush and some candy. The rest was for groceries that we needed. About three miles from home, old Dan ran away. We set our feet in the egg basket for a brace both pulling as hard on the lines as we could. But the shaves of the buggy came loose, a wheel hit a post and tore off the rim first. We lost Grandpa Roy and the egg crate and all the eggs, then the buggy cushion, next the buggy. Then I was hung to the lines, so the horse drug me up the hill on my back. Finally, I got the lines from around me. Then it was just the horse and shaves, so he stopped. Grandpa Roy came running to see if I was hurt. He caught the horse; we took him back to the buggy, left the shaves and harness and led him home. He was broke to ride but we didn't ride, we walked. We weren't bad hurt. But it cost quite a bit to have a man named Mr. Dancbee (a blacksmith) in the community to fix the buggy.In the meantime we had to walk to school.

In 1937, I believe, Grandpa Roy got a job up at Clayton, New Mexico. He had a V8 Ford car (black). He can tell you what work he did there. Your Grand Mother Grace Gholson Humphries graduated from the U of N.M. college the same day that Grandpa Roy did.

After a two or three year courtship, they were engaged and married in June 1938, I think. In 1942, on February 26, your daddy, Leroy John Humphries was born. From here on he can tell his story.

Your Great Grandpa Humphries still lived on his ranch with great Aunt Alma to help him with the cattle and she took care of him.

All these years since Grandpa Roy went away to work at Clayton, New Mexico, great grandpa had still been raising pinto beans for his money crop and corn and cane for the cattle and hogs. First he farmed with horses, then with mules. In the 1930s, he bought a four-row Case Tractor. He first kept one hired hand then another to do the farming after he got too old.

They would hitch up one unbroken mule and one gentle mare and hook them to a homemade two-wheel cart. Drive them around on the school section until the mule learned to pull the cart and to guide. So that time the team got scarred at something, Great Grandpa was driving, he had the lines. He decided he'd better jump off, so he did, taking the lines. Grandpa Roy stayed on the cart. This was about 1926 or 1927. Of course, the team jerked the lines causing great Grandpa to fall and skin all the hide off of his face as he slid in the dirt and gravel. He jumped up and went running after the cart and team. He was afraid for Grandpa Roy. But the team came to a fence and as a mule will not run into a barbed wire fence, he stopped but the mare run into the fence. Grandpa Roy jumped off and got the lines. Up came G. Grandpa as he dashed up, he said, why didn't you jump off son? Grandpa Roy looked at Great grandpa and said "Looks like you'd have been better off if you had stayed on too, Dad. For blood was dripping from G. Grandpa's face where he'd slid on the gravel.

Once in 1933, I believe, when the crop was laid by, Grandpa Roy decided we'd take a trip for Great Aunt Alma's birthday, as she'd always worked so hard for us all since our mother had died. He decided we'd just go to see Kentucky, our parents birth state. We'd heard so much about the beautiful blue grass country, the tall timber, two-story white houses and all kinds of fruit growing. But Great Grandpa said I'll just stay here, you kids go. I might get sick if I went back East. Now if you were going west I'd like to go further west. So Grandpa Roy said, OK, then we'll go west. We've never taken a trip altogether, so we'll go by El Paso, see part of Old Mexico, go by Las Cruces, Lordsburg and on to Arizona. Visit your old neighbors, the Guy Beedles at Globe, Arizona; go see the Grand Canyon, the Petrified Forest.

Author's note: this is the last page of thirty-one handwritten copies that I have, did they go west? Maybe some of you know or want to guess.

Iva Humphries, my mother's (Jeannette Piggott's) best friend and neighbor in New Mexico was one of the sweetest persons that I have even known. When we would visit her in the 1950s, we would be in awe of the beautiful handmade quilts that she had made.

All three of the Humphries girls/women were extra special; very kind and gracious Christian ladies. Although, I do not ever remember meeting Roy, their brother, who lived in Albuquerque, he was very popular (according to my mom, Jeannette) and well liked.

Iva eventually married Leonard Hobbs. They had two children Pansy and Harold. Harold was killed in an automobile accident when he was in high school at Corona.

The Humphries

by Grace Humphries Lackey
April 15, 1981

In response to the request of my son Daniel, I will attempt to put on paper, some of the history of our families, the Lackeys and the Humphries.

There will be no fiction, *it is* all true facts.

I do not know very much of my grandparents, but will put some I do know down.

I should know much more about Grandmother Ethel Lackey's people, but have forgotten a lot of what she told me. Maybe some things I repeat may make you remember more of what she told you, and you can add that in too. For she is the one grandparent you all, even to many of my grandchildren, had the privilege of getting to know and be around. I've had fifteen years to get started on this. If I had written one hour a day, look how much I would have done.

LOST
Two golden hours
Each set with 60 diamond minutes No reward is offered
For they are gone forever

The parents of Grace Humphries were John Wesley Humphries and Nora Ellen (Wright) Humphries. The parents of John Wesley Humphries were Sam Humphries and Linnie (Humphrey) Humphries.

When I was a very little girl, instead of fairy tales or TV my favorite story was, "Mama, tell me about when you were a little girl."

My grandmother's maiden name was Biddie Ann Swim, my grandfather's name was Jack Wright. They were married quite young, Grandmother was thirteen, Grandfather was nineteen. They built themselves a little log cabin on their land in Kentucky, two or three miles, I guess, from Hilda and Smile, two little towns. I remember mama getting mail with that postmark. I don't know how they got their land but probably it was a claim. They had twelve children, Johnny and Jasper were first. Grandmother had a very good dog that watched over them while she worked in the field. They raised corn, potatoes, and tobacco. Johnny ate green apples and took dysentery and died, Jasper died, but I can't remember how. Jimmy, Mary, and Marshall were next, then Lawn, Martin and Helen, then Annie, Paulina and Nora Ellen (Ellie, they all called her), and a baby that died real tiny. Uncle Jimmy married and moved to a farm some distance away, I don't know how far, far enough that Grandpa and Grandma didn't get to visit him. He kept asking, they just couldn't get away, so he wrote them he was on starvation. The next day they got hams and fruit and everything they could think of to take him, left the little children in care of Uncle Marsh and his wife, got on their horses loaded with food and went to Uncle Jimmy. Before they got there they noticed fine clean fields of fine corn and tobacco. When they got to his house they found he had a lovely home, orchards, garden and a delicious supper ready, but Grandpa was so

Grace and Paul Lackey, 1936.

mad, because his son had tricked him after the good bringing up they had given him, he wouldn't get off his horse, he was going home. I don't remember how they got him in a good humor, but they stayed two or three days and really enjoyed it. While they were gone their kids at home took over—they decided the house needed cleaning, they moved everything outside and camped out while they cleaned. It seems like it rained, the calves and pigs got in the orchard, they had a terrible time, but had everything under control by the time the folks got back.

Of course, the family had outgrown the log cabin long before this. They built a new house. I used to love to hear Mama tell of the building, but I have forgotten the details, but she did help lay the stone for the fireplace and chimney and helped put the shingles on the roof. When they built the new house, there was a spring in the northwest corner of the yard. A few feet south of this spring was a large flat rock, they built a little house over this rock, they called it the springhouse. The ice-cold spring water ran over this rock. They would set their big crocks of milk, bowls of butter and anything they needed to keep cool on this rock.

In the winter Licken River froze over until they could drive a team and wagon over it. They built a little house they called the icehouse, it was a few feet west of the big house. They made it double walled and put sawdust from the sawmill in the wall then they put a layer of sawdust on the floor. Then they cut big blocks of ice from Licken River and hauled it up. They put a layer of ice and another layer of sawdust and so on until the house was full. This ice lasted them way into the summer.

There was a dug well behind the house by the kitchen door. It had a big rock on top of the curb with a big hole. I don't know how they got the hole there, but they drew water out of the well through this hole.

Mama and Aunt Pliny had a path through the little hills to go to church. Uncle Mart got them each a little lantern to carry so they had light on dark nights. On Wednesday nights they had prayer meeting in the homes. The children would play outside while the grown folks had their prayer meeting. One night it was at Mama's home, they were all playing. They decided to playa game called, "I will throw, but who will wind," a girl would throw a ball of twine and a boy was supposed to find it and wind it up, one girl threw it and it kept unwinding, all of them were back together, by then they got kind of scared, they went in a group following the twine. It had somehow landed in the old log cabin and a goose had her nest there and got that twine and kept unwinding it.

The old women met for a sewing circle at different homes, so when it was at Mama's home, her brothers Lawn and Martin decided they didn't want to see them old women, so they put rosin on their eyes. They figured they had made a big mistake by the time they got it off for it had pulled out their eyelashes and their eyelids were sore.

One day Uncle Mart brought Mama two baby squirrels. She named them Jackie and Julia. Something happened to Jackie, but she had Julia a long time. She would sit and hold Mama's yarn while she knitted. One day there were some men working and when they came in to wash, one of them put the tin wash pan over Julia. She walked around until she heard Mama's voice and went straight to her and Mama took the pan off.

As Grandfather and Grandmother grew older and the older children married, Mama and Aunt Pliny did most of the outside work. They had to haul the wood and plow the fields with oxen. Aunt Annie worked in the house. Grandma and Grandpa both died when Mama was thirteen, so Uncle Marsh and his wife and family moved in to take care of the girls. Aunt Mary was married and had a family of her own and lots of times on the way home from church they stopped and ate Sunday dinner with her.

Uncle Lawn was married with a family, one daughter especially loved to visit Aunt Ellie. They would go fishing in Licken River. One Sunday Ida wanted to go fishing, Mama said, "You are not supposed to fish on Sunday, listen to that bird." Sure enough it sounded like the bird said, "Don't fish on Sunday, don't fish on Sunday," so she didn't ask anymore.

Uncle Martin was killed when a tree fell on him. Aunt Annie married, lost her first baby and died when the second one came. Aunt Helen died at eighteen with what they called "galloping consumption." I imagine it was pneumonia.

Aunt Pliny married. I can remember Mama getting a letter telling her Aunt Pliny had died when I was six or seven years old. Mama and Aunt Pliny (Paulina) were close pals like Grandmother Ethel and Aunt Sally. (My cousin Vina that I write to is one of Aunt Pliny's daughters. Iva used to write to Elizabeth or Lizzy and Mary Cooper is the one that came to see us for just a few minutes one day. There were two boys, Simpson and Luther. Luther loved Aunt Ellie and held the wagon wheel when Papa and Mama were married (he thought he could keep them from going.). I remember Mama going behind the house and crying. I was always at her side, we sat on the dirt shelf Papa had piled up all around the house, I cried too, I didn't know what I was crying for except Mama was crying, so it had to be bad. Do you remember the boards and dirt around Grandpa's house where Aunt Alma and Aunt Iva and I used to plant flowers? It was to keep the cold winter wind from blowing under the house and coming up through the floors. Do you remember it was covered with tarpaper? It used to be black then they put new paper on and it was green.

Now back to Kentucky, so this left only Mama at home. Uncle Marsh still lived at the old home place. His trade was to make brooms and tombstones. Then when he got a lot made, he and his wife went to sell or deliver them. This left Ellie (Mama) at home to take care of their children. They had six sons. They also had six daughters, but all died in infancy except one. She lived to be two. She was Mama's pride and joy and it broke her heart when she died.

Uncle Marsh worked on his brooms and tombstones way into the night and Mama had to hold the lantern for him. She would get so tired.

Uncle Marsh lived to be up in his eighties, he preached for years and still lived on the old home place. We went to see it when we went to Archie's wedding.

When I first remember, I lived in a little house with black tarpaper. It was my home and I loved it. My big sisters (Alma and Iva) and my brother Roy were all in school. They had to walk to the school two miles straight west. I remember them telling things that happened. I didn't know what a spelling match was, but they laughed and told Mama, one boy Bob White, spelled "needle," "n-i-d-d-l-e," and the teacher said, "It does not have an 'i' in it." He responded, "Well it's no good then." The boys played leap frog (a game) and a big boy let Roy fall and break his collarbone. They played blackman, little white house over the hill, baseball, basketball, and when there was snow, fox and goose. To me it was like a story, they always told the funny things. One Easter, they were invited to an Easter egg hunt. Roy came home and said, "Mama, there is a new family and they have all girls and you know they have twins and you know, there is two of them twins."

I thought it would be nice if I could go, but I was too little, so I always stayed home with Mama, but we had good times. She let me help plant the garden, feed the chickens, she taught me to sew, and I got to go to the store with Papa and Mama and my little friend Anna Belle lived there. She always had so many pretty things to play with, and one time she gave me a yellow cat. I named him Tom. I enjoyed him very much, but not so much as I had my kitty Maud who took the sore eyes and Papa carried her and her six kittens off. I can still see them stringing out across the pasture on the way to an old barn where Papa thought they could find mice. I never saw her again. I don't know how long I had had her, but seems like a long time. She would let me dress her up in doll clothes and she would stand up in my little red rocking chair and hold one of my rag dolls.

I also got to go with Mama and Papa after wood. I got to put small pieces in to fill up the holes, so I thought I was helping.

Papa had an Uncle Willis Humphries who lived over close to the Mesa. Edna and Charlie Gonce now own his place. Once or twice a year at least we got to all get in the wagon and go visit him. He had a beautiful team, they were dark bay with blaze faces and jet black mane and tail. I don't know what Papa and Roy and Uncle Willis did, but the first thing, he would kill a hen and dress her for Mama and put on lots of water. Then Mama and the girls would wash all his bedding and wash and scrub his floor and get dinner. I mostly played, he always saved all the bottles and cans and I played house. He had a big black dog I just loved too. One time we went to pile beans for him, I was about nine then, so I worked too, but I somehow had a little time to play. This time he was living in what he called his winter house. It was a half dugout. The top part was made of flat reddish pink rocks. When we got ready to go home, he always had five or six bottles of green pepper sauce for us. He used the vinegar, but didn't like the peppers. We liked them in our gravy with bacon or ham. That is the last time I ever remember visiting Uncle Willis. He also came to visit us lots of times. He would stay all night with us sometimes. One time he brought us a little brown and white puppy he found on the road from Willard. He gave it to Ellie (Mama). He was her dog, he would do anything she needed him to do. She would say, "Rover, go get those calves for me" and he would go get them, bring them in to water, and when they were finished all Mama and I had to do was guard the end of the lane and he took them back to the pasture, but if we kids tried to get him to go, he sat down wagged his tail and opened his mouth as if to say, "You go, I'll go with you," and he would, but not alone like he did for Mama. He was my pal of course, everywhere I went, but when my kittens were little he would grab one and shake it to death. He was jealous and I sure got mad at him. When they were older, he paid no attention to them.

After I was married and moved about two miles away, he would come over stay two or three days or a week with me and go home. He was sixteen when he died.

When Uncle Roy was in about the third grade, anyway he had the *Story of Gulliver's Travels* and he couldn't say Gulliver, one of our mares foaled. The colt was tiny and white and he wanted that little colt so bad, Papa told him, you learn to say "Gulliver" and she is yours. He learned to say "Gulliver," and named the little colt Fly. She was so gentle I learned to ride her. So I called her mine because she was getting old and Roy had some of her colts to ride to round up horses and cattle.

There were not many aeroplanes in those days, but one day Fly was tied to the yard fence, a little plane came over so low it scared her and caused her to break loose from the fence. One night she came up to the lot gate and Papa found her dead the next morning. She had come up to get doctored I guess. She must have been at least fifteen years old.

I had several rag dolls Mama had made for me, all of them had names and I loved them all. One day Uncle Roy traded me out of two of these for five cents each. After a few days I grew lonesome for my dolls and wanted to trade back, after some time he finally consented. He was always teasing me so when we went out in the backyard and he began digging, I thought he was teasing, but pretty soon he began bringing out pieces of my dolls in scoops of dirt with the posthole digger.

One year it was very dry, we had to cook great pots of split beans and rabbits for our hogs and chickens. Roy caught the rabbits in traps.

When I grew old enough to go to school, I felt real important. The first night all the others had lessons to get and I wouldn't go to bed until I had studied too, so Aunt Alma set me a copy of numbers up to ten. I don't know how good I did, but I was satisfied. The teacher's name was Mr. Dunlap. He was a young man and had no patience with little folks. Alma had taught me to spell my name fast, so when he called me up and asked me to spell my name it sounded like this, "Gracy Chump Chias," (Grace Humphries). He decided I had to sit with Alma so she could make me behave. I talked out loud and whispered.

The next year, for six weeks, we had Ruth Dean, a pretty blond girl, for the younger children. Then I guess they gave out of money for we had to go into the other schoolroom with the big children. Mrs. Ward, Lorene's grandmother, was the teacher. Lorene was my dear friend I had known since we were two and three years old. In the afternoon when we got tired and wigglesome she sent us out to play.

One day we walked to school. I don't remember how it had been when we started out, but after dinner a storm came up. Mrs. Ward saw that it was getting worse. It was from the east. A school bus came from the Center Valley community, over north of Cedarvale. The bus driver came early. Mrs. Ward had the big boys make a good fire in the big heater and she shut it off good. Then she wrote a message real big on the blackboard, "Mr. Humphries, we have taken your children on the school bus with us. We will let them off a mile east of your house so they will not have to face the wind and snow. Uncle Roy stayed with his friend, he had permission to spend the weekend with him. That left we three girls to walk alone. Alma walked in front, Iva behind her and me behind Iva. We made it just fine, the wind helped to push us home. Sure enough, Papa had saddled up old Fly, wrapped up good and Mama put a piece of net window curtain over his face. He did fine going over, he read the message, warmed good, then started home. He had to face the blizzard for two miles, he had to get off and walk, he got so cold, but Fly knew the way home, so they arrived safe. There were icicles on Papa's mustache; the veil was a sheet of ice. We were all safe and warm at last.

The next year Mr. Maxwell was our teacher. He had a nice little wife. They lived in the log schoolhouse across the doorstep from the frame schoolhouse we attended. He was a real good teacher. It was close to Christmas, he had our program all planned and we knew our parts and songs. Martha and I sang "Jolly Old Saint Nicholas," Iva and some of the other girls were to be Negroes, all blacked up eating watermelon in their imagination. They first sang "What I Wants Mos' for Christmas." Oh, real thoughtful like, then they sang, "A Water

Melon Big as So," and measured with their arms, Yum, Yum, Yum, a melon Oh. We practiced it all over, some men brought in a big tree and set it up in one corner, the old organ was in another, there were two book cases, a big wood heat stove, lots of seats all arranged. We were all ready for our program. It was a nice day. We all went home. Our program was to be on Christmas Eve. Before that time came we had a big snow, but we weren't about to miss that program. Papa and Roy put bows on the wagon and covered them with horse blankets. They put bean hulls in the bottom of the wagon and Mama heated big rocks. We all wrapped up good and away we went. Everybody in the country was there. Our program went off fine and we had our gifts and the tree was all decorated pretty.

The next day Mama fixed us a big fat hen and dressing, sweet potatoes, coconut cake and fruit salad and I don't know what all else. After dinner was over and the dishes were done, everyone reading or resting, Iva and I slipped into the kitchen and picked all the nuts and bananas out of the fruit salad that was left. I don't remember getting scolded.

We always raised a garden and Mama had plenty of fresh vegetables for us in the summer and canned beans and cucumbers and beet pickles. We raised lots of good sweet turnips and cabbage. Papa would dig big holes and bury them in the fall so they lasted all winter. We also had lots of pumpkins and onions. We didn't have a cellar so they covered those good in the smokehouse. Sometimes at Thanksgiving time and sometimes it was Christmas vacation, we would kill four or five big fat hogs. We ground lots of sausage and seasoned it, then we would pack it in little long sacks as long as the flour sack Mama made them from and as big around as she wanted the sausage to be. They hung in the clean corncrib until they were used up. We cut the fat all up into small pieces and Mama rendered that into lard and poured it into clean buckets. The hams, shoulders, and sides of bacon were trimmed to perfection, Papa saw to that himself. Then he hung a big box by strong wires in the barn. A layer of salt was put in the bottom, then a layer of hams, then a layer of salt rubbed in good, then a layer of shoulders, then a layer of salt rubbed in good, then the bacon or middlins as we called them, then more salt. Then they hung there six weeks. Of course, he checked on them all of the time, and added more salt when necessary. When the six weeks were up, the meat was taken out and the salt scraped off, then we laid each piece on a clean piece of old sheet, shirt, dress or old apron and sewed up nice and tight to keep any bugs or dirt out, then we dropped one ham or shoulder etc. in a clean gunny sack, wired its top and it was hung in the corn crib until it was used. It usually lasted us all winter and all summer.

We saved all the fat scraps and trimmings that were not good enough to use in beans and in the spring while it was still cool Mama and Papa built a fire in the water lot where it wouldn't catch the wood pile afire. They put a big black wash pot on the fire and added so many gallons of water, so much lye out of a can, and the meat scraps, They boiled and boiled until the meat was all eaten up by the lye and it began to thicken, they beat it and stirred it then let the fire die and the next morning it was ready to cut out in to cakes of soap and lay in the barn to dry. The only time we bought soap to wash with was when the lye soap was all used up, then Mama would buy P and G soap. I don't know how many pots they made. I also made lye soap to wash with until all these powdered soaps came in, then I stared buying them as we quit raising hogs, because we couldn't raise corn anymore because it was so dry.

In the winter of 1918 and 1919 many people took the flu. I don't know if all or part of my family had it, but I did. I was two years old and I remember distinctly of setting up in bed and crying for "egy." Mama's hens were not laying so Papa rode horseback three miles to the little store, they had two eggs, he bought them both and paid fifty cents a piece for them.

It was so cold the cattle died. They froze to death standing up. Cattle were not very high priced in those days, but Papa lost $2000.00 worth. He didn't have any sheds. They had never had a winter like that. That is the reason he built the big barn that still stands on the old Humphries ranch. Mama kept me in the house, but I remember seeing Papa, Alma, Iva and Roy come in nearly froze from skinning the cattle to save the hides. They would eat a good hot dinner and go back. I don't know how long it took them or if they skinned all of them.

The railroad track was one mile north of our house. We could see the New Mexico Central (name of the train) go by every day. We loved to hear it whistle. One winter the snow blew into the cuts along the railroad until the train was stuck. I could watch the men working around it from Mama's bedroom window. It was very fascinating to me. Then they finally put a little car, we all called the Do Dad, or "Dinkel," everyone had their name for it, it was about like a school bus is now, only it was black and run on the rails. I remember in 1929 we met Mrs. Piggott, Jeannette, Martha, Viola, Bertie Lee and Jimmy at Progresso. They had come on the Do Dad instead of a train.

It sure seemed lonely when the tracks were taken up. The Highway 42 now runs north of the old home place where the track used to be.

I always considered Iva my pal. I guess that was her job to take care of me. One day she gave me some buttermilk. I wanted some more. I called it, "butty mic." She thought that was cute so when Papa and some other men came in she wanted me to say it for them, I remember she put me in the high chair my feet just stuck off the edge of the seat, so I must have been about two, anyway I wouldn't say butter milk for them, she kept on until finally I said "I ain't agonna say ole butty mic anymore." Of course they all laughed because I had said it for them. Iva and I had picnics, went after the cows, and learned to whistle through our hands. It seems we were always working together. When it was gardening time, housecleaning time or canning time, I was the errand runner, watched the birds off the garden, fed the baby chicks, carried the hogs wallow, got the cows milked, cooked if they needed me to. If I had a good book to read, I put it under my jacket and sometimes stayed longer at an errand than I should have. Sometimes while ironing or housecleaning Iva and I would persuade Alma to read to us; then we were all happy. Iva and I both loved cream, so if Alma sent us to the house to get dinner, we got us a bowl of corn flakes and cream. We always wondered how she knew it, she would holler and say, "Girls, get out of that cream." Years later we asked her how she knew. She said, "That was easy, one of you always kept watch at the window."

Papa and Roy did the plowing, planting, and cultivating. We girls did the hoeing.

We would get our housework and chores done, sometimes get something started for dinner, take our water in a tin syrup bucket and walk to the field. I was the hoe sharpener. We always had our file stuck between the post and the wire at the end of the field. 1t was about one-half mile to the fields we walked to, the others Papa took us to in the wagon, some times we took our lunch, otherwise the girls got dinner while I fed the chicks and watered the hogs. One year the field we called the middle draw was so thick with weed it took us half a day to make a round, one row apiece, six rows to the round. The little bean plants were so spindly we could hardly tell them from the weeds. Papa told us if we hoed that field the beans off it was to be ours. So we hoed it and it rained, the beans came out good and really grew. Then a new crop of careless weeds came up and covered them up again, but when we went to pile the beans we knew it wasn't weeds we were lifting. Papa stacked them by themselves. The others stacks were so pretty and shiny, you could see the big bean pods, but ours looked like a stack of weeds. When the thrasher man came, he said "I don't want to thrash those weeds." Papa said, "If you won't thrash that stack, you won't thrash any of my beans, so he thrashed it. It just turned to beans. We got sixty sacks out of that little stack. He sure was surprised, he was a Finn, his name was John Jockey, he said, "Mr. Humphries, I thrash all your weeds." In those days one man owned a big thrashing machine, it took a big crew of men to run it, the farmers in the country all went together from one farm to the next and all worked on each others' thrashing, each one paying the other back for helping him, but the man that owned the thrashing machine got paid.

The next summer was dry and nearly all the neighbors left to get jobs. Wrights, Gustins and Beedles all went to Arizona. Piggotts went to Kansas. There weren't enough children to have a school, so the superintendent at Willard, Mr. Ferguson, came down and brought Alma a report card for me and said she could teach me. I was in the fourth grade. We used Martha Piggott's books from the year before. In those days the books were not furnished, the parents bought them. Roy was in the ninth grade, Iva in the eleventh grade and Alma in the twelfth grade, so they missed that year. Alma was a good teacher. I had to learn my lessons or I studied them over again. Some days I was all through by noon. Some times it was dark, or after supper when I finished. There were not many of those days. Roy had a trap line and Mama, Papa, and Iva picked twenty-one sacks of beans for seed. When Roy didn't have to ride his trap line, and Alma and I had our school over we all picked beans. Roy got tired of my studying and reciting out loud so he called it a blab school.

Mama pieced quilts, Roy and Papa got the harnesses all mended for spring plowing, Iva crocheted or tatted and I played and Alma would read books and continued stories out loud to all of us. We really had a happy winter together.

The next summer wasn't so dry. We did have some crops. Before time for school to start Papa and Mama went to Willard. They rented a house from Dr. Ottison for ten dollars a month. It had five rooms and two porches. Mama thought it was real nice. She was so happy her children were going to school. Then she got sick. She had pneumonia; in those days they didn't have the medicines they do now. On November 5, 1926, she left us. She had gone to her reward, but it was a lonesome terrible time for all of us. Rover howled and we couldn't stop him. He knew his dear mistress was going to die.

Papa went ahead and moved us to Willard after the crops were all in as they had planned. He said, "Now Norie wanted you kids to have an education, so I intend for you to get it." That left Papa all alone. Every other Friday night he drove in the wagon to see us. He came home on Sunday afternoon. Rover always came with him. So you can imagine how scared we kids were when Rover arrived one weekend all alone. I think we saw a neighbor in town that said Papa was

OK. After that Rover came lots of times all by himself to see us kids. When spring came Uncle Roy took his finals early and moved home to help Papa plant. Then when school was out they moved us girls home. Then we had the garden to plant, the house to clean, the hens to set and be all through so we could hoe. Aunt Alma graduated in 1927, Aunt Iva in 1928, and Uncle Roy in 1930, and I graduated from grade school. Early in the spring of 1930 while I was studying for state exams, we all had a siege of measles. Aunt Iva first, before she got well, Uncle Roy took them, then Aunt Alma and I went down at the same time. Papa had a Spanish lady do our washing otherwise we took care of each other. I still got well in time to take my state exams and passed. Only three of us didn't have to take any over, so the teachers rewarded us by letting us take a class of basket weaving. I still have my little basket.

After Alma, Iva, and Roy had all finished high school, Papa and some of the other men finally got a school bus route started. Howard Gustin bought a two-seated car. That was our school bus, and by holding the little kids on our laps and a little wee seat Howard made on each side there were ten of us who rode in that car. Howard drove until he and I were through high school and a few years after, I don't know all that part.

My senior year was 1934, and on our senior trip, our class and two teachers went to Carlsbad Caverns. It was free then on Governor's Day for seniors. We had a great time.

The Lackeys

Grandpa William David Lackey had two sisters and three brothers, Uncle John, Uncle Bob, Uncle Walter, Aunt Ella, and Aunt Lizzie. When he was little, his father had to go to war, World War I. Uncle Bob's wife's name was also Ella, they had one son, Archie. Our Archie is named for him. Until Grandpa was twenty-one he stayed with his parents and helped them. Then he said, Papa, I'm going to get my education, so he went out and herded sheep for a man to make money to go to school. One day he was out with the sheep and a storm came up. He saw a live oak tree and thought he would get under it out of the rain. About twenty steps before he reached it, lightning struck and shattered it, throwing pieces of wood all around him.

He would board with some family. One of them was the Jollys. He was there when Mrs. Jolly died. They had a son in New Mexico, but they didn't know how to get in touch with him. Years later after they came to New Mexico, he met this son in Corona and told him he had helped bury his mother. The son was a real old man by this time, he wept when Grandpa told him about his mother.

When Grandpa started to school in the third grade at age twenty-one, the other pupils were little folks and he was a grown man, but he learned rapidly and took two grades each year. He finished the eighth grade. In those days that was a good education. One of his teachers was Professor Hunter.

When he was in school, there was a smart aleck rich boy, always spouting off.

One day he and Grandpa got in a fight, Professor Hunter made them cut down a live oak thicket for punishment. They did, without speaking to each other. When they were old men, they met again and had a good visit.

Grandpa Lackey owned and ran a store in Paint Rock, Texas. A young cowboy came in one day griping about the squatters, etc. Grandpa said, "Young man, do you know what you would have to eat if there weren't any squatters as you call them, you would eat beef and rawhide." The young man said, "No, I hadn't thought of that."

Great Grandfather Owens was in the Revolutionary War. He was buried in Yancy

County, North Carolina. Grandpa Owens was six years old and when they shot the guns at the funeral, he thought they were shooting his daddy.

Robert Lackey was the grandfather of Will Lackey (our grandpa).

Thomas Abercrombie lived at Grapevine, Texas. He was a veteran of the U.S. vs. Mexico War. He was Grandma Ethel Lackey's great uncle.

William Jasper Lackey was born in Tennessee in July 1833. His father was Robert Lackey. His mother's maiden name was Hawkins. One brother John Lackey, one half-brother Robert Bicknell. Robert Lackey died when William was four or six years old. William Jasper Lackey entered the Civil War in 1862. He was in the twelfth Louisiana Regiment Company K, Hood Brigade. He was out on furlough when the war ended. William Jasper Lackey was married to Nancy Ann Smith 18 _ 9, nine children were born, two dying in infancy. Almeda died about 1902. William David Lackey was born November, __ , 1862. Lizzie, Robert, Eller (died Feb. 1904), John, Walter. W.D. and Lizzie all born in Jackson Pariah, Louisiana. W.D. Lackey moved to Arkansas with his parents at seven years of age. He came to Texas at eight years of age with his parents.

Children of Joseph Owens born 1812 and Epsey Gunter Owens born 1812 were Aunt Pernice married Chambers and had no children, Father William Riley Owens born July 7, 1834, and died November 22, 1921 first marriage to Narciss Wilson and had nine children by first wife, second marriage to Mary Florence Abercrombie and had seven children by second wife, Aunt Caroline married Charlie Davis, Doc Owens died in infancy, Ann Owens Pierce had two children Jack and Jeff Pierce she died when second child was born, Jane married Emory had four children, Uncle John Owens had four children, Geraldine Cole had Fanny and Sallie then when her husband Mr. Cole died she married a Baptist preacher Bro.Hendon and had two children Mennie and Bulah.

James Gideon Abercrombie, November 20, 1823–1904, married Sara Elizabeth Hull born in 1822. Their children were Aunt Eliza Jane Willingham, Aunt Rose Ann Cullins, Uncle Hugh Abercrombie, Aunt Angie Elrod—one child Leota, Uncle Jessie Abercrombie, Uncle Drew Abercrombie, Aunt Belle Bailey.

Mama Florence Abercrombie born April 2, 1862, in Oxford, Alabama, died June 20, 1926, at Cedarvale, New Mexico, married William Riley Owens in Bryant, Arkansas, September 7, 1884. Their children were Ethel May Owens Lackey, Christeen died at four years old with diphtheria, Sallie Wallace, Ida Herring (they had one baby boy, Raymond, died at one year old), Bly Walton, and Fay Ross.

Grandmother Ethel Lackey dictated the following to Grace Lackey in about 1968. Children of James Gidion Abercrombie and Sarah Elizabeth Hull Abercrombie.

1. Eliza Jane- Married Isack Willingham 2nd Fisher, three sons, Walter, John and Thomas and one baby girl.
2. Rose Ann- Married George Cullins, Sarah, Ethel and several other children, I don't know their names, one boy was John.
3. Angie- Married Frank Elrod, one child Leota, Aunt Angie married an Adams later.
4. Jessie- Married a Ruth, but I don't know her surname, and they had several children, but I don't know their names.
5. Mary Florence Abercrombie- Married William Riley Owens in Bryant, Arkansas, September 7, 1884. Their children

1. Ethel May Owens, August 1, 1886
2. Christeen Edwards Owens, Dec. 24,
3. Sallie Effie Owens, Aug14,
4. J da Owens, July 5, 1891
5. Bly Owens, Jan. 30,
6. Fay Owens, Feb. 10, 1896

7. Harry Raymond Owens
End of dictation.

When Grandmother Florence Owens lived close to Little Rock, she walked over a mountain to school and the ticks stuck to her stockings.

Harry Raymond Owens was buried at Deep Creek Cemetery in Wise County about four miles from Boyd, Texas. He died at the age of about one year, two months, with dysentery. Christi Edwards Owens was buried at Cooper Creek Cemetery about five miles from Denton, Texas. There used to be a church house there. This grave used to be covered with mussel shells. She died with diphtheria at the age of four years.

In 1907, charter members Mr. and Mrs. W.R. Owens, Mr. and Mrs. Henry Davis, Claude Collins, and Fannie Copeland organized a church named Bliss near Sterling City, Texas. Bro. Lanford held a meeting, Bro. Staten Coleman. Will Lackey, Ethel Lackey, Sally, Ida were converted and baptized and joined. This paragraph of information provided by Ida Herring September 15, 1976.

Lackeys and Owens

Ethel 1886, Christie, Sallie 1889, Ida Lee 1891, born three miles from Denton County, Cooper Creek, Hassie Bly 1894, Denton Creek, Faye February 10, 1897, Raymond December 1898 Denton Town lived two years. Buried February 1900 in Wise County, Deep Creek Cemetery. Denton County to Weatherford, Texas.

Grandmother Ethel Owens Lackey oldest daughter of Florence and W.R. Owens was born August 1, 1886. She had five sisters, Aunt Christy died with diphtheria when about three, Aunt Sallie Wallace, Aunt Ida Herring, Aunt Bly Walton, and Aunt Fay Ross, and one brother who died in infancy with dysentery at about one year old. Grandmother Ethel helped take care of her little sisters. Of course, they had lots of fun and lots of troubles. One day Aunt Ida fell and broke her arm, when they were putting her to sleep to set it, she said, "I've melt it enough, I've melt it enough, I've melt it enough." She was always afraid of blood, one day Grandma and Aunt Sallie put some beet juice on her for fun, she really thought she was hurt bad. One morning Grandmother Owens was out milking, somehow Aunt Fay turned Grandmother Ethel's dishwater over on herself and scalded her real bad.

They lived close to Denton and Decatur. When the courthouse was being built in Denton, Grandma climbed to the very top of the tower, lots of steps, she loved to tell about that. I think Christy and little brother Raymond are buried at Clear Creek, where they lived. The Clear Creek place was seven miles from Denton. There was a ravine with pecan trees. Grandpa Owens cleared a place under some big pecan trees so Grandma, Aunt Ida; and Aunt Sallie could pick up pecans. Later they moved to Miles, then finally on west. Once they went back to see Grandmother Abercrombie in Alabama. They went swimming in a creek, which turned out to be polluted. Grandmother Ethel took the typhoid fever and nearly died. All of her hair came out. Jeff pierce, Mr. Owens' nephew even brought the team and wagon over so they would have it to haul her to the cemetery, but she got well. Her hair came back in real curly. She lived on chicken broth and buttermilk. Grandmother Owens rubbed and bathed her lips. She learned to walk again. She was sick ninety days. When she was strong enough they went back home to Texas.

One year 1899, they went to visit Mother's folks in Little Rock, Arkansas, and lived with Aunt Lizza Fisher, Mother Florence's sister. Ann was Mr. Owens' sister.

Jane Emory was Mr. Owens' sister. Then they came back to Weatherford, Texas. Aunt Fay and Aunt Bly had typhoid. They stayed in Weatherford a year, then went to Wise County, Decatur, and Boyd. There is where brother Raymond died and was buried. From Wise County they moved to Fort Worth to Miles, Texas, in 1901 in west Texas. Stayed about a year moved closer to Miles. Arm Townson House, went to school one year, moved to Concho County close to Paint Rock in 1903, seven miles from Paint Rock. Ethel and Will met in Carl Schlinkey's field where Will, Ethel, Ida, and Sallie were picking cotton. Will had Mr. Schlinkey's place rented.

Will and Ethel were married January 1, 1904. Mrs. Schlinkey gave them a big supper and dance. They were married in the late afternoon. Grandma Owens fixed a big supper then they all went to Schlinkey's to a dance then supper at midnight.

They lived on Schlinkey's place in a new little house the first year. The next year they lived on the Ranchburger place until the fall. They bought a quarter section and built a half dugout on the divide (where we visited). The folks moved up on the divide in 1905. They all moved together.

Will and Ethel moved in 1910 to John Chapman's place. Then they moved on the White place where Paul was born in 1911. The same year before Paul was born, Grandma Owens was in a team runaway and broke her all to pieces and Mr. W.D. Lackey was working on a place to put a bridge in that day. They wanted him to work in the courtyard. There was a big cave-in, Grandma thought Grandpa Will was in the cave-in so she had another scare.

Will ran a store in Paint Rock, Texas, and ran a mail hack also. The mail route was from Bliss to Sterling City.

Grandpa Will Lackey ran a mail route with buggy and mare before he was married between Lana and Lampassas. One time he started to cross a river. The river was so high it took the mare and buggy downstream, dumped the mail bag out, so Will pulled off his new boots, held them in his teeth and swam in and got the mail bag (he lost his boots). A doctor lived close by. He had a boat so he took the mail and Mr. Lackey across to the other side, the other mailman and sack was there, they exchanged mailbags so the other mailman could go back. This mail route had been robbed down in the canyons several times. One moonlight night as Papa drove along, two men on horseback rode up, one on each side of the buggy, they didn't speak, and just before they got to the canyons, they rode on ahead. Papa started through the rough country put the mare in a lope and fired his six-shooter several times into the air. He always thought they had intended to rob him but changed their minds when they found out he was ready for them. When Paul was nine months old they moved to Austwell in 1912. In 1915 they moved to San Angelo, where Grandpa Will took pneumonia. He got half his insurance because the doctors said he wouldn't live, so they took their money and bought a team and covered wagon and started for New Mexico.

In Conclusion

Throughout reading these personal recollections, I was often surprised by the reporting of simple but very detailed incidents—events that would seem not to have any particular relationship to the story being told. These events, however, remain solid images that are passed down through the generations by the telling of stories; our oral histories. Several other things caught my attention, the number of children who died young and the awful illnesses with which they were afflicted. But, by contrast, the number of persons suffering from respiratory illnesses that improved due to the climate. My favorite stories were about the amazing pets, each one referred to by their given name, from horses to squirrels, they were special.

The harsh reality of these times seemed to foster affection and caring for one another; their families and their struggling neighbors. They hung together. They worked with and for each other. Times were tough but they took time to play; to socialize, to learn and to worship.

I am most grateful to those who generously took their time and their efforts to frame some pictures in our minds of life in the early 1900s in the New Mexico area.

And so, we bid you adieu.

Old Piggott Ranch. (photo courtesy Gary D. Atkinson, 2006)

Bibliography and Sources of Information

1. Fray Angelico Chavez History Library and Photo Archives Santa Fe, New Mexico
2. *Ghost Town Basketball* by Steve Flores

New Mexico Histories

1. *The Fabulous Frontier* revised and enlarged edition by William A. Keleher
2. *Glimpses of the Ancient Southwest* by David E. Stuart
3. *New Mexico* revised edition by Calvin A. Roberts and Susan A. Roberts
4. *New Mexico's Troubled Years* by Calvin Horn with a foreword by John F. Kennedy
5. *The Spell of New Mexico* edited by Tony Hillerman

www.ingramcontent.com/pod-product-compliance
Lightning Source LLC
LaVergne TN
LVHW061249100826
845148LV00008B/1072